The Parish that Disappeared

A History of St John's, Hereford

The Parish that Disappeared

A History of St John's, Hereford

by

Liz Pitman

Logaston Press

LOGASTON PRESS
Little Logaston Woonton Almeley
Herefordshire HR3 6QH
logastonpress.co.uk

First published by Logaston Press 2016
Copyright © Liz Pitman 2016

ISBN 978 1 906663 99 5

Typeset by Logaston Press
and printed and bound in Poland by
www.lfbookservices.co.uk

*Front Cover: an extract from Timothy Curley's map of Hereford of 1858
(photographed by David Lovelace)*

To all those people who have helped me make Hereford a very happy home –
you know who you are!

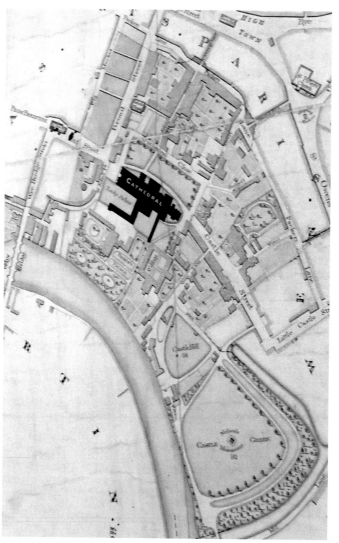

The area of the city around the cathedral, part of which formed the core of the parish of St John's, shown on the Tithe Map of 1840. For the actual parish boundaries see the maps on pages 2 and 3.

CONTENTS

Acknowledgements .... *ix*

Foreword .... *xi*

Introduction .... *xii*

1   Beginnings to the fall of the West end in 1786 1

2   Life in the Parish to the fall of the West end 19

3   From the fall of the West end
      to the dissolution of the Parish 29

4   Life in the Parish to its dissolution 41

5   The Silversmith, the Recluse & the Bank Manager 55

6   The Clairvoyant, the Manure Manufacturer
      & the Dancing Master 63

7   The Slave Owner & the Governess 73

8   Epilogue 89

Appendix: List of Parish Vicars 91

Bibliography 93

References 97

Index of Names 107

General Index 111

ACKNOWLEDGEMENTS

Thanks are due to many people. First and foremost I would like to thank Rosalind Caird, the former cathedral archivist, who was extremely generous with both her time and knowledge, making many useful comments and suggestions on the text. David Lepine also acted as a most helpful and courteous mentor. Thanks also go to Jo Henshaw, formerly Cathedral Close Project Learning Plan Manager; Marianne Percival, formerly local studies librarian; Anne-Marie Dossett and Lauren Price, all of the city library. Rhys Griffiths and Elizabeth Semper O'Keefe, of Herefordshire Archives, were also helpful at a difficult time for the archives. The cathedral Chancellor, Canon Christopher Pullin, PJ Pikes, Ron Shoesmith and David Whitehead have all made helpful comments on the pre-Reformation chapters. All the staff in the cathedral library were helpful in various ways, in particular, Gordon Taylor the cathedral photographer, who was tenacious in sorting out many of the images included in the book. To those people who read early drafts and encouraged me to go on writing, I owe a real debt of gratitude. I am grateful, in particular, to Nick Baker, Bob Clarke, Ursula and Tom Davies, all of whom made useful comments on my draft text. Alison Warren, Delia and Peter Harris and Joy and Thomas Roderick were enormously helpful as constructive critics and proof readers.

Thanks also go to: Wendy Brogden, who supplied me with material on parish recusants; Stephen Butt for information on Barnardo Eagle; Henry Connor, who gave help on several medical topics and on Andrew Rowan; John Eisel, Miriam and the late Michael Webber for material on Solomon Lazarus; Lady Ann Hoskyns for material on Chandos Hoskyns; Michael Hunter, Curator of Osborne House, for his help with the alleged Queen Victoria link; Mrs Ann McCabe, who owns the original Dovey diary; Elizabeth Patrick for material on the Pritchard family business; Cornwall Record Office for permission to use the Gertrude Dziewicki letters; Howard Tomlinson for information on Herr Goetz; Ewa Kotewicz for help with Gertrude Dziewicki's Polish life; Peter Thorpe, National Railway Museum, for his help with Bradshaw's timetable; Christine Gladwin, Sidcot School, for information on Gertrude Dziewicki's time there; Phil Bufton, Hereford Family History Society, on Gertrude Dziewicki's headstone; Jennifer Milligan, for information on the Quaker members of the Dziewicki family and Sue Jones, Leominster Priory, for help with Severin Dziewicki's tombstone.

I also owe a debt of gratitude to the Castle House Hotel in Hereford and its staff who, when the weather was good, were happy to let me sit in their tranquil garden and work on the draft of this book. Finally, I thank those friends who have patiently listened to me as I recounted yet another 'find' – whether it was Gertrude Dziewicki and her Polish adventures; George Barnardo Eagle, clairvoyant and 'wizard of the south'; or the hatter turned manure manufacturer, Andrew Rowan, who was not only charismatic and intelligent but also, perhaps, something of a wide boy.

Any omissions and errors in the text are entirely mine.

Liz Pitman
March 2016

FOREWORD

Until the beginning of the 19th century there were just 17 cathedrals in England. They fell into two categories: monastic and non-monastic. The former were cathedrals run by monastic orders, usually Benedictine, such as those of Durham, Winchester, Norwich and Worcester. The latter, known as secular foundations, were cathedrals run as colleges of priests, with Hereford, York, Lincoln and St Pauls, London being examples. Many of these had parish churches associated with them, but few ran as parish churches themselves.

In the 19th century, with the development of the industrial north, many new cathedrals were established, becoming known as 'parish church cathedrals'. These were buildings that had been major parish churches but which retained their parish status and geographical area when being elevated to cathedral status.

Hereford enjoyed all these various permutations of cathedral and parish. It had an altar in the cathedral which was associated with a geographical parish, named 'St John the Baptist', thus being a parish without a church, but with residents who, by long custom, worshipped in the cathedral.

For many years, this unusual anomaly worked well: a priest, usually a member of the vicars choral, was appointed, with responsibility for the cure of souls within the parish boundaries. By the time I arrived in Hereford in 2002, the anomaly was becoming rather acute. I was appointed, as had been several of my predecessors, as 'priest in charge' of the parish of St John, but the parish boundaries had been so reduced in the preceding 100 years as to make the notion of a parish an anachronism. We found ourselves with all the appurtenances of a parish (parochial church council, churchwardens, and representatives on Deanery Synod) but with no financial or pastoral responsibilities.

By 2012, it was felt that the time had come to regularise the situation and, after long consultation, the parish was finally abolished. As a community, we 'beat the bounds', symbolically, for the last time, in June 2012. Several important things have been retained, however, not least our association with St John the Baptist. The cathedral community 'beat the bounds', symbolically, for the last time, in June 2012. Several important things have been retained, however, not least our association with St John the Baptist. While the parish under his patronage may have been abolished, the cathedral still honours John as one of our patron saints.

The passing of the parish also opened our eyes to its long and venerable history and we owe a huge debt of gratitude to Liz Pitman, who has worked tirelessly to delve into the archives. Liz has produced a fascinating story of human and ecclesiastical eccentricity – the lives and loves of the people who inhabited this geographical area and her stories are such as provide a real-life rival to those of Trollope in *The Barchester Chronicles*!

I hope that this volume will provide interest and delight as we remember this special part of Hereford's past.

Michael Tavinor
Dean of Hereford

INTRODUCTION

The parish of St John the Baptist in Hereford, with its altar inside the cathedral, was probably founded early in the 12th century, surviving until 2012 when it was dissolved.[1] As such, it had a much longer history than any of the other parish altars once found in four of our secular cathedrals.[2] Nine hundred years of history is a long time, yet, in the index to the official *History of Hereford Cathedral*, the parish 'church' of St John has only 19 entries. Since this piece of cathedral history has disappeared with barely a whisper, it seemed a good time to reflect on some aspects of its past. Indeed, it is curious that its long and fascinating history has, to date, excited so little interest. In this book I hope, in some small measure, to redress the balance.

Whilst, at some level, it would have made sense to divide the story into the pre- and post-Reformation period, the lack of material before the 18th century and the wealth of material after it make for a better balance with a split in the late 1700s. The book is therefore divided into three parts. Chapters 1 and 2 trace the history of the altar and the parish until the 18th century, taking the fall of the west end in 1786 as a cut-off point. This fall was not only an architectural upheaval, but a practical one as well, when what was seen as 'the vexed issue of how to deal with the parish of St John' became a continuing problem for the dean and chapter.[3] Chapters 3 and 4 cover the same topics from the time of the fall to the dissolution of the parish church when, on 17 May 2012, it was agreed that the 'benefice and parish of St John shall be dissolved'.[4]

Chapters 5, 6 and 7 tell the story of some of the characters who emerged from the pages of census returns, newspapers and archives during the course of my research. Most of the people of the parish, like so many ordinary people throughout history, have disappeared without any trace of their lives, but some parish residents seemed to demand that their stories be more fully researched. I have, in general, concentrated on the unknown residents, rather than the clerics and more eminent men and women of the parish, as many of their lives are already well documented. I have also included interesting parishioners who would not have been part of the cathedral community, but who simply lived in the parish – the Jewish Solomon Lazarus and the Catholic/Quaker Gertrude Dziewicki.

There are many gaps in the parish story, particularly in the early history, and this book cannot pretend to be a fully comprehensive history. However I hope that the stories in this book bring to life something of the rich history of the parish, with medieval and Dickensian squalor rubbing shoulders with clerical and civic splendour.[5] Truth, it is said, is stranger than fiction and the stories I discovered, full of life, humour and sadness, certainly endorse the truth of the adage.

1 BEGINNINGS TO THE FALL OF THE WEST END IN 1786

> One oddity was that the parish church of St John was actually located within the cathedral, even though the parochial services were disrupted by (and disrupted) the services in the cathedral choir.[1]

Introduction and origins

The story of the early centuries of the parish and its 'church' within the cathedral is a difficult one to tell as records are scarce and it is easy to feel that the parish was, at least until more detailed records begin, almost invisible. As a result its early history, beginning about 900 years ago, has to be fleshed out partly by a series of questions with tentative answers rather than definite facts.

The first question to be asked is: 'When was the parish founded'? Hereford had been a diocese with a cathedral since Anglo-Saxon times. A stone church built by Bishop Athelstan (c.1015-56) was at the least severely damaged when, in 1055, Aelfgar, son of the earl of Mercia, who had been outlawed by Edward the Confessor for treason, raised an army of mercenaries against the new earl of Hereford, Ralph the Timid (so-called because of his apparent hesitation in taking action). The army sacked the city, burnt the cathedral and killed some of its canons. At that time, the parish system was still evolving and the pre-Conquest minster, in the absence of parish churches, would have had a significant pastoral responsibility for the spiritual welfare of the laity of the town, including the rites of baptism, marriage and burial. By the time the Norman cathedral was built (between about 1107 and 1148), parishes, each with their own church and vicar, had become the norm, but in the centre of Hereford something unusual happened. What must have been a survival from its earlier history occurred when a 'designated parochial altar seems to have arisen during the transformation of the old Saxon minster'.[2] A parish was carved out of the area around the cathedral, making it one of the earliest parishes in the city, with only St Peter's, c.1080, and St Owen's, c.1101, being earlier foundations.[3]

The new cathedral became the place of praise and prayer in which the round of daily masses occurred, with the parish altar serving the cathedral laity and other people living nearby.[4] However, from the inception of the parish, references to its vicar always refer to him as serving at the 'altar of St John', suggesting that the dean and chapter were at pains to emphasise that there was only ever a parish altar in the cathedral and not a parish church.[5] Given the dignity of cathedral worship and the more hurly-burly life of a socially mixed parish, it is not perhaps surprising that the history of the relationship between, on the one hand, the parish vicar and his parishioners and, on the other hand, the dean and chapter seems, on many occasions, to have been marked by tensions and disagreements.

*Timothy Curley's map of Hereford of 1858 with the area of St John's parish
around the cathedral outlined in green*

If the parish was created when the new cathedral was built, its first century of life is unrecorded, as there is no written or architectural evidence about it, but, as soon as written evidence is found, the history of the parish, albeit still with many gaps, begins to emerge. The earliest written reference occurs *c.*1201, when 'William of St John, and Hugh, chaplains', witnessed a deed relating to a piece of land being granted as a dowry to Helisend, the daughter of William Albus de Hereford.[6] This same William, 'canon and chaplain of St John', who was living in King's Ditch (King Street), witnessed several other undated 13th-century deeds relating to land transactions.[7] In addition, the 13th-century cathedral statutes stated that the cathedral treasurer must 'provide light for all who celebrate at the cathedral, with the exception of those who are celebrating at the altar of Saint John'.[8] Certainly, by the time the *Taxatio Ecclesiastica* was compiled in 1291, St John's was treated as a parish.[9]

The main part of St John's parish was closely linked to the area known as the bishop's fee, that part of the city under the jurisdiction of the bishop rather than the king. Within his fee the bishop had considerable privileges, with his authority sometimes exceeding that of the civil authorities. Although the boundary of the two fees was ill-defined, it is likely that in Anglo-Saxon times the area within the city defences marked out the bishop's holding, and, when the parish of St John was formed, it followed this boundary line.[10] By Norman times this area consisted of the cathedral Close, the east-west roads of Castle Street, King Street, West Street, East Street and, running north to south, Church Street, Broad Street and St John Street, with

2

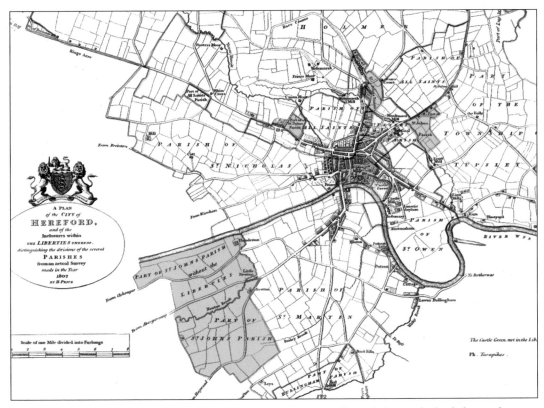

Price's 1802 map of Hereford with the various parts of St John's parish shaded in red

Gwynne Street and Wye Bridge Street running down to the river. The castle was also part of the parish but Castle Green was outside the city liberties. From the early days of the parish, there were canonical houses in Canon's Row (the Close) for, by 1321, they were already being described as 'old'. Other canonical houses could be found in Caboche Lane (Church Street) and Castle Street.[11]

A second question to which there is no definitive answer is why, as with other city parishes, there were areas that were detached from the rest of the parish but included in it. These outlying areas were at Blackmarston, Hinton, Newton, Hunderton, Widemarsh and Canon Moor (so called as cathedral canons held three hides of land here),[12] the first four being south of the river. Several cathedral dignitaries already held land outside the city by the time of Domesday.[13] Hunderton and Hinton were clerical holdings by the mid-13th century, and it is highly likely that the other areas were also cathedral property and thus allocated to the parish when it was formed.[14] However, a contrary view is that these areas were 'added at a later date [after the foundation of the other parishes] in a rather arbitrary way'.[15] This view was reinforced when, in the early 20th century, the boundaries of the original parish were being greatly reduced. The cathedral sexton, Mr Alban Moore, commented, perhaps rather sardonically, that 'it was an old joke that when the city was mapped out, St John's was forgotten and afterwards the odds and ends were allotted'.[16] Joke it might have been, but it could, nevertheless, have had a grain of truth in it.

3

A third question is: 'Why did the dean and chapter site an altar inside the cathedral and create a parish around it, rather than building a separate church for its laity's needs'? Again, there is nothing in the records to give a definitive answer but a look at the composition of the area that became the parish possibly holds some clues. Finances and population, or rather lack of them, might have been the reasons. Hereford was 'one of the poorest of the secular cathedrals' and this poverty might have influenced the decision not to build a separate church.[17]

As for population, a parish needed to be able to support both a priest and a church, but, as with so much else in the early history of both cathedral and parish, the records do not give any clear information about who worshipped where. There would have been a relatively wealthy clerical population, including the men associated with diocesan administration and the 28 resident canons who lived in the canonical houses nearby. These men were expected to maintain households of some style and substance and to provide hospitality and lodgings for important senior members of their households, who were often younger members of gentry or leading urban families.[18] These men would have needed clerks, servants, stewards and washerwomen. In addition, grave diggers, carpenters, plumbers, glaziers and others would have been amongst those working for the cathedral and its clergy. Goldsmiths and painters were also needed, for the cathedral was much more highly painted and decorated then than it is today. Masons working on the fabric of the new cathedral would also have been plentiful. Many of these people could well have had homes or lodgings in the parish. In addition, the blacksmiths, fletchers, soldiers, armourers and others serving the nearby castle would probably have lived in the parish. Yet, despite this varied populace, it might not have been sufficiently large or wealthy enough to warrant the cost of a separate church with its own vicar, for the clergy would usually have worshipped in the cathedral, leaving only *hoi polloi* residents of the parish to attach themselves to the parish church.[19]

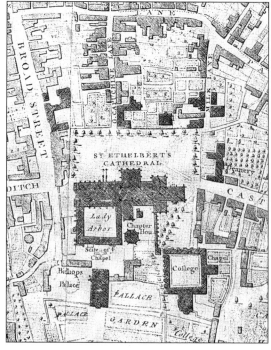

Another reason for the lack of a church might simply have been lack of space. The new cathedral was going to be a large building in the centre of an area that already had a nearby castle as well as houses and a burial ground for the whole city in the Cathedral Close, an area bounded by Broad Street, Castle Street and Canons Row. It was an area that was already filled 'with trade, industry, housing and religion' and it is hard to see where, in this crowded space, both above and below ground, a parish church could have been built.[20]

It has been suggested that the cathedral, in the course of its 12th-century rebuilding, might have 'swallowed up a small adjacent church of St John'; an idea that gained some credence in the 1650s, when Silas Taylor, a prominent Parliamentarian, found some 'stupendous foundations' near the cathedral.[21]

Isaac Taylor's 1757 plan showing the cathedral and the Close

4

However, these were far too magnificent to have been part of a parish church and they were most likely to have come from the Saxon cathedral damaged in 1055. They might even have been the foundations of either a bishop's or a royal palace, for Hereford was, from Anglo-Saxon times, a royal centre.[22] It therefore seems safe, given the complete lack of evidence for a separate church, to conclude that one never existed. The question of building a separate church dogged the history of the parish throughout the centuries, but it never happened.

The final question with no clear answer is that of the whereabouts of St John's altar within the cathedral at the time of the foundation of the parish. Again hypotheses abound, with both the crypt and north transept being possibilities. The crypt, completed around 1220, was probably meant to provide a better setting for the cult of St Ethelbert, but it could also have provided space for worship for the parish of St John, with the steps leading into the crypt from the Close allowing parishioners to come and go. However, there is no written evidence for its ever having been the parish church and although these steps provide some slight architectural evidence, as it was not built until some hundred years after the probable foundation of the parish, it still leaves open the question of the original position of the altar.[23]

Another view is that the parish altar of St John was first situated in the original Romanesque north transept. It seems likely that 'at least the return for walls [of such a transept] had been built well before being rebuilt in the mid-13th century' during the episcopate of the wealthy, but unpopular, Peter de Aigueblanche.[24] It would have been this transept that the antiquarian John Leland saw when he visited Hereford around 1530, writing that, when Bishop Swinfield translated Cantilupe's bones to the north transept in 1287, it was to the 'the chapel of the church of St John'.[25] Rather in the manner of Chinese whispers, many centuries later, George

Thomas Cantilupe's shrine as it may have appeared c.1287

Marshall also wrote that Thomas Cantilupe's remains were taken to 'a new tomb to the north of the altar of St John in the aisle of the north transept'.[26] If the parish altar was there when Cantilupe's tomb arrived, the latter would have been the interloper, rather than the parish altar. Sadly, none of the written references, dating from the period before Cantilupe's translation, mention the actual site of the altar.

If the altar was in the north transept when Cantilupe's bones were interred in 1287, it is very likely that it was swiftly moved to another part of the cathedral, for, by the end of the 13th century, many pilgrims were coming to the cathedral in order to pray for a miracle at the shrine. There must have been rich pickings for those non-clerical people of the parish who met the needs of these visitors. They would have needed food, drink and, sometimes, lodgings or medical care. There was at least one physician and, when the pilgrims relaxed after their vigil at the tomb, they could be entertained by a 'harper and a mimer who would drive away cares'.[27]

As well as pilgrims thronging the cathedral, there would be the murmuring sound of the many daily services, sung mainly for the glory of God. Although lay people were not strictly necessary for this *opus dei*, secular cathedrals actively sought worshippers and masses were scheduled in such a way that there would always be a service for any passing laity.[28] These services were performed by the vicars choral whose chief duties were the 'recitation of the seven canonical hours and the celebration of the daily high mass'.[29] Masses for the dead would also have been celebrated at the many cathedral chantries.[30] As for the parish, how many services were held is not known, but it would have been to their parish altar that people turned for spiritual well-being and the rites of baptism, marriage and burial.[31] It is easy to imagine that these parishioners, most of them poor, illiterate and unkempt, would have caused some concerns for the dean and chapter. In his version of the *Doctrinal of Sapyence,* a treatise aimed at instructing 'symple prestes … and simple people', William Caxton complained that, during services, people would often wander about, misbehaving by 'spekyng in lawhing [and laughing] and many other maners'.[32] The cathedral must have been a veritable Babel and the parishioners seen, perhaps, as more of a nuisance than a gift.

As there was only a parish altar, it would not have had the furnishings of a conventional parish church, although the cathedral's Norman font would have been used for parish baptisms. However, medieval piety and devotion were such that parishioners would probably have made major contributions to the upkeep of the chalices, candles, vestments and the other items necessary for both the altar and its clergy. Glimpses of these items can be found in gifts made to the parish, as in a bequest, dated 1267, made by Robert Le Grant of a large book of legends of the *Lives of the Saints* given to the altar of the parish church of St John.[33]

The nave of Hereford Cathedral in 1833, the black arrow marking the site of the altar of St John

However, it is not until 1394, over a hundred years after Cantilupe's burial, that the first definite evidence about the place of the parish altar within the cathedral occurs. Records at that time state that the parish altar, which would have been one of many medieval altars in the cathedral, was 'near the entrance to the choir and at the back of the dean's stall'. It must, however, have been a nuisance for the cathedral clergy, for Bishop Trefnant complained that:

the chaplains, clerical and lay [of the parish], when singing the psalms and chanting in their rough manner, inflict such discord and senseless noise on those chanting in the choir that … great danger is occasioned to those celebrating and grave scandal to the hearers. We bid you, in the desire for the peace and quiet of those serving God, and wishing to avoid scandals, to inhibit Sir John[34] who says that he is vicar of the altar of St John … to cease chanting while the ministers of the choir are singing or ministering, under pain of excommunication.[35]

Despite this dire threat of excommunication, the vicars of St John must have largely ignored it, for 20 years later, the dean, John Prophete, 'on account of his affection towards Hereford cathedral, proposed to construct a chapel of St John in the south part of the cathedral … so that when the chapel was completed mass might be said with less disturbance.'[36] But the project fizzled out; the chapel was not built and the stonecutters probably found themselves either out of work or engaged on the general building work going on in the cathedral.[37] The altar was still in the nave in 1536, for, when Bishop Foxe was asked to certify the value of the ecclesiastical benefices in Hereford, a vicar (unnamed) was listed as serving the parish of St John at an altar in the nave.[38] The parish altar then seems to have stayed in the nave until being moved to the choir in 1767.

From the 13th century to the Reformation

St Thomas Cantilupe as depicted in a stained glass window, Credenhill, Herefordshire

The city of Hereford reached the highest point of its medieval development in the 13th century with the splendours of the cathedral, several other churches and a Jewish synagogue. Although not an overcrowded city, it would still have been a bustling, smelly, noisy, place. There would have been open stalls selling meat and fish in the market, animal droppings on the streets, the cries of vendors selling their wares and carts lumbering through both city and parish.[39] However, the parish might have been something of an oasis of calm, for several houses had gardens or land used for the cultivation of vegetables, herbs, fruit, flowers and even saffron.

The 14th century was full of challenges for both city and parish. In 1315 and 1316, there was famine 'brought on by torrential rains, general crop failure and livestock murrains'.[40] These harsh years were followed in 1348 by the Black Death, when up to half the parish population died.[41] For those parishioners living in close proximity to the cathedral and its burial ground, the times must have been terrifying. The stench of death would have been everywhere, for bodies from all over the city were brought on carts and dumped, several at a time, probably none too ceremoniously, in the plague pits at the west end of the Close.[42] Yet, only a year later, on 25 October 1349, when the bones of Thomas Cantilupe were taken to the Lady Chapel from the north transept, death and ceremony were close companions, for 'King Edward III, the lords of church and realm, and the people of Hereford gathered in the church, where the bishop consigned into the hands of that

7

formidable saint the protection of his church in times of plague.'[43] However, as the Close was the burial ground for the whole city, problems continued well after the plague years. Forty years later, in November 1389, Richard II granted a licence to the dean and chapter 'to enclose the cemetery and lock it at night to avoid in future the spoliation of the goods of the cathedral church, the burial of children at night without baptism, the exhumation of corpses by swine and other beasts, and other immoralities.'[44] Despite the presence of nearby gardens, the area around the Close must have been a less than pleasant place in which to live.

The Black Death as depicted in the Toggenburg Bible of 1411

Life in the parish was not all famine and plague, however, and after the Black Death there was another period of economic prosperity for the city, with the revival of the wool and cloth industries. Other signs of affluence could be seen in the continuing work on the cathedral and other city churches. Living as they did so close to both the castle and the cathedral, parishioners would have enjoyed the spectacles that occurred when important people, including royalty, visited. In 1486, for example, Henry VII's visit was the excuse for an elaborate pageant within the cathedral, in which St George, St Ethelbert and the Virgin Mary all had speaking parts.[45]

The men who became the parish vicars were normally members of the vicars choral.[46] Appointed by the dean and chapter, this vicar would usually combine his parish duties with continuing service as a vicar choral, as can be seen from the accounts for the canons' bake house in the late 1300s which, on a regular basis, refer to the vicar of St John receiving 1d a day for 'ruling' the choir.[47] The names of several of the pre-Reformation vicars are recorded, but little else is known about them since sources of information about 'these minor clergy are much more elusive than the canons'.[48] They would probably have had a limited education although, as vicars choral, they would, at the very least, have had a working knowledge of Latin, and have learnt 'by heart the psalms,

Hereford Castle, from the model of the medieval city displayed in the Old House Museum, High Town, Hereford

the antiphony and the hymnary'.[49] Many would have been local men.[50] William Credenhill, for example who, in 1363, was named as the chaplain at the altar of St John, might well have hailed from the Herefordshire village of the same name, whilst John Baker alias Salwarpe would have been a Worcestershire man, as Salwarpe is a small village in that county.[51]

As a parish priest, the vicar of St John's was responsible for a variety of services. Mass would have been held on Sundays; with 24 June, the date of the festival of St John the Baptist, being a cause for major celebration. Canon law stated that the laity had to hear mass in their parish churches and to receive penance and Communion at least once a year, usually at Easter. The parish priest would have educated his flock in the Christian faith, ensuring that they had some knowledge of the Ten Commandments and the seven works of mercy, virtues, deadly sins and sacraments. Much of his teaching would have been illustrated from the 'poor man's bible' to be found in the stained glass and wall paintings that would, in medieval times, have been the norm in both cathedrals and parish churches. He would also, of course, have been responsible for baptisms, weddings and burials.

Although some events in the late middle ages barely touched the diocese, these early vicars would, nevertheless, have been running their parish against the backdrop of turbulent religious and political times. William, the first named chaplain of St John, would have been affected by King John's quarrel with Pope Innocent in 1208. He placed England under an interdict after John refused to accept the pope's choice of William Langton as archbishop of Canterbury. Churches were closed, masses ceased to be said, and 'the gathering together of the faithful … was forbidden, and only the barest essentials of baptism and burial were allowed'.[52] By 1334, Robert de Hanwelle was the vicar of St John's. Whether he was still the vicar at the time of the Black Death of 1349 is not known, but whoever was incumbent then could well have died. The number of deaths for Herefordshire clergy soared from just four in 1348 to 56 in 1349. In the parish, with the cathedral and burial ground at its heart, nearly a third of the canons died with, presumably, similar losses amongst the vicars choral.[53] All clergy would have risked infection as they tended to the needs of their sick and dying parishioners and when they died 'the celebration of masses, visitations to the sick, burials of the dead, and comfort to the poor' would all have been affected.[54]

The first vicar about whom a little more is known is a Benedictine monk, Brother William Bradley, originally from the monastery of Alcester, in Warwickshire, who was named in a tax return of 1407 as serving the altar of St John. He became a *cause célèbre* since, in that year, several of the cathedral canons took his case to the archbishop of Canterbury. They complained that John Mey, the city mayor, believing that William Bradley was guilty of theft, had ordered two of his henchmen to enter Bradley's room in the cathedral cloisters. There they found some stolen stock fish (cod and other fish cured by splitting open and drying in the air), together with a dagger, a bow and six arrows, which the owner had lost a few days before. Although William Bradley does seem to have been a thief, the canons felt that sanctuary had been invaded. However, the archbishop said he would not impose a penance as long as the items were returned. This was agreed and thus 'concord was restored between the canons and the mayor'.[55]

By 1423, William Maxey was the parish vicar. He was granted a lease for life 'while he was vicar of the altar of St John, and for one year after his decease' of a 'house near the gate of the canon's bakery … a shop annexed to the said house … and a parcel of garden'.[56] William Maxey

James Wathen's sketch of May 1799 with the vicarage house (on the right) at the end of Castle Street

must have led a comfortable life there, tending his garden when not tending his parish. We get another glimpse of him when he was involved as an escort to the bishop's prison. In medieval times, clerics who broke the law were tried by the consistory court and would then find themselves in the bishop's, rather than the city, prison and, in 1422, William Maxey was one of the men ordered by Robert Haliday, the vicar general, 'to convey to the bishop's prison all clerics convicted before secular judges'.[57]

Another dishonest vicar followed on from William Maxey. In 1444 Roger Rogers conspired with some local laymen to defraud the dean and chapter. Between them they subtracted, during the years 1438-42, tithes owed to the value of ten marks. The dean and chapter won the case and Roger Rogers and his dishonest cronies had to pay both the subtracted tithes and the cost of the suit.[58] After this, little is known about the parish vicars until 18 years into the reign of Henry VIII when, in 1527, Thomas Brystow, curate of St John's, was reprimanded, along with four other members of the vicars choral, 'for failure to attend the offices'. As a result rules were laid down 'for their discipline, subsistence and general supervision'.[59]

The Reformation years

By the time that Thomas Brystow was being reprimanded, England was facing the political and religious upheavals of the English Reformation. Henry VIII was about to set in train his challenge to the religious status quo as he began the long-drawn out battle for divorce from his first wife, Katherine of Aragon. Yet the early years of the Reformation scarcely touched the diocese and the parish clergy and parishioners who, in this relatively remote part of the country, continued going quietly about their local, unreported lives. In 1534, with the Act of Supremacy, Henry declared himself the Head of the Church of England, thus precipitating a break with the pope in Rome. Although nothing is known about the vicar of the parish at this time, he would have had to swear an oath acknowledging royal supremacy over the church and renouncing the jurisdiction of the papacy.[60]

By the time of Henry's death in 1547, the Protestant church was in the ascendancy, although Hereford was to remain Catholic in its sympathies for a long time to come. The centuries of masses in Latin, of celibate priests, of highly painted and decorated churches, were coming to an end. The following years were bewildering in their changes, first to a much more hard-line Protestantism with Edward VI, then with a return to the Catholic faith with Mary I. It was not until the pragmatic Elizabeth I became queen that a more stable period began in cathedral and parish life.

Edward VI was a mere 9 years old when, in 1547, he became king but, with a Protestant education and a conviction that he was to sweep away the last vestiges of popery, in his brief six year reign he ushered in drastic changes in religious reform. In 1547, cathedrals were ordered to 'destroy utterly all shrines … candlesticks, pictures, paintings … and images found in stained glass windows'.[61] The conservative cathedral did not acquiesce and it may not have been until May 1550 that Thomas Cantilupe's shrine in the Lady Chapel was taken down.[62] Stone altars also had to be removed and, although it is not known how far this order was complied with in Hereford, it is possible that the parish altar was replaced by a wooden one. Only two candles were allowed on this wooden altar, which would have had had an English Bible set up on it. In 1552, when the second Book of Common Prayer was introduced in Hereford, the way was paved for a service in English in which the laity could participate, and in which the strict segregation of the priest from the congregation disappeared. Nothing is known of the vicar of the parish, or indeed of the reactions of parishioners to these changes, but St John's altar, remaining where it was in the nave, would have offered a spiritual sanctuary to people in rapidly changing times. Whilst people might have lamented the loss of Latin, with its sonorous beauty, it must have been a revelation to parishioners, most of whom were illiterate, to hear services expounded in their own tongue. The Catholic Eucharist now became the Anglican Communion, preaching became increasingly important and morning and evening prayers overshadowed the communion service. Parishioners were commanded to receive communion at least three times a year, including Easter. By the time of Edward's death in 1553, ordinary people were still digesting these sweeping reforms but, with the accession of Mary I, Edward's devoutly Catholic half-sister, another religious change swept through the country.

In Mary's even shorter reign, there was a reversion to Catholic practice, which was probably welcomed by Hereford's rather conservative clergy and populace. With such rapid changes in the religious life of the country when, in 1558, Elizabeth I became queen, she inherited a Church in which a good deal of confusion prevailed. Although her religious reforms could be seen as a classic case of taking the middle ground, they nevertheless resulted in hostility and attempted rebellion from both the Catholic and Puritan elements in the country. In selecting her bishops, Elizabeth chose those sympathetic to her reforms and for Hereford she selected John Scory, a former Dominican friar who had become an adherent to the Protestant cause.

Scory found that the cathedral 'was a verie nursery of blasphemy, whoredom, pryde, superstition and ignorance' and that 'all but one canon were dissemblers and rank papists'. Even the cathedral sextons were 'mortal enemies to this [reformed] religion', as were the members of the city council. Indeed Hereford had become a magnet for disaffected conservatives where 'priests and suchlike enemies of the church find a safe asylum ... and are maintained and feasted as if they were god's angels'.[63]

In 1559 royal injunctions, as part of the religious settlement, were sent out throughout the realm. Those for Hereford included injunctions relating to the regulation of worship, the reading of scripture, the placing in the cathedral of 'two bybles of the largest volume in Englyshhe' and the 'relyve therwith [of] the poore wayfareinge honest & nedye persons'. It would seem that the clergy also needed injunctions about their personal behaviour 'because there ys nothinge more abominable in goddes sight than adulterye and fornication and other suche filthy lusstes', so women were not allowed into their chambers. In addition the vicars were to avoid 'scorneful words ... theire conversation shall be honest without contention vertuous gentle learned and tending to the edification of others.'[64] The lack of complete records for the period mean that the vicar of St John's is not known but he would have been included in this general demand for seemly moral and spiritual behaviour.

The 1558 Act of Supremacy meant that the vicar of St John's would have had to swear an oath of loyalty to Elizabeth as supreme governor of the Church of England. In the same year the Act of Uniformity made attendance at church for parishioners once a week compulsory, with a fine of 12 pence for those failing to attend divine service.[65] Those who refused to conform were most usually Catholics who became known as 'popish recusants'. Elizabeth, as a pragmatist, initially took a moderate stance towards recusancy, but, after various plots against her realm and her life and despite her best efforts at religious toleration, she was forced to take ever harsher measures against Catholic recusants. They could, for failure to attend divine service, be forced to remain within five miles of their home, fined and, if they failed to pay the fine, imprisoned. It must have taken a good deal of courage to continue as a recusant in the face of these punitive penalties, yet many people did, including some of the parishioners of St John's. In 1591, Philip Skynner, who had been the vicar of the parish since 1588, presented 28 parishioners for not communing at Easter. Although the most common punishment was a fine, five of these parishioners were excommunicated, a terrible punishment for ardent Catholics, who believed that this would put their souls in peril.[66] However, quite often leniency seems to have prevailed, as in the case of Richard Legge who, although fined, did not have to pay as he was a pauper.[67] Perhaps the authorities knew when they were beaten, as trying to get money out of a pauper would have been a waste of time.

Elizabeth died in 1603 and, with her death, also died the Tudor dynasty. The first Stuart king, James I, inherited a country in which recusancy was still a problem. Such recusants were seen as traitors, particularly after the Gunpowder Plot of 1605 when fanatical Catholics tried, but failed, to blow up the king and parliament. In 1605, William Jones was charged with 'abusing the vicar in the church with unseemlie speeches and for not receiving the communion for four years and for teaching without licence'; Elizabeth Brooke was 'a common brawler and swearer and blasphemer of God' who did not go to church; John Ballard abused the churchwarden and called him a rascally knave.[68] These recusants were seen as 'ruffians' for, as well as swearing and brawling, they committed other offences, such as selling goods on Sundays and feast days or playing tennis, presumably also on a Sunday. Perhaps these brawling, law-breaking recusants were not so much concerned about purgatory and damnation after death, as with enjoying this life first.

It was not only recusants who got into conflict with the ecclesiastical authorities. Members of the vicars choral were also admonished about behaviour unbecoming to a cleric. One such vicar choral was John Boughan, who became the vicar of St John in 1605 after the death of Philip Skynner. In 1610 he was accused of adultery but, although he admitted spending time in an ale house with the wife of John Nicholson, he denied having 'any private conference or company' with her.[69] John Boughan seems to have remained vicar throughout the reign of James I and into the early years of Charles I, dying in 1629.

From Civil War to the Glorious Revolution

Charles I became king in 1625 and, with the help of Archbishop William Laud, attempted to introduce rules on matters of ritual that were seen, in particular by Puritans, as favouring Roman Catholic doctrines. Whether or not the parish vicars had Laudian tendencies is not known but something is known about the pastoral work of Jonathan Dryden who, by 1636, was vicar of St John's. He seems to have been a man of principle and compassion, as his petition to the mayor and justices on behalf of some poor children gives us an insight into his charitable work. He explained that there were, in the parish, 'many poore children whose parents are no wayes able to bring them up, and as he believes that he is bound by virtue of his pastorall charge to take care of the poore to his best power' he entreated the justices 'to commend these poore children as apprentices to able men'.[70] The names of 13 children were appended but, sadly, the records do not tell us whether or not his petition was successful. Jonathan Dryden clearly had a second string to his clerical bow as, in the same year, he was charged with 'keeping swine within the gates of the city'.[71]

The period of the Civil War and the Interregnum which followed (1642-60) was another confused and difficult time for Hereford. In 1645, the city was captured by Colonel Birch for Parliament. Shortly after his success, the canons were ejected from their houses, 'the other buildings in the Close were seized, and the college [of the Vicars Choral] was assigned to the homeless poor.'[72] In the same year, the Book of Common Prayer, seen as too 'popish' for the new Puritanism, was replaced by the Directory for Public Worship. Communion still occurred but worship was centred on the reading of scripture, prayer and lengthy sermons. A year later, *An Ordinance for the maintenance for preaching ministers in the city and county of Hereford* stated that six 'able, godly and learned divines, named by the Committee of Plundered Ministers' were to be appointed to the city, of which three were for the cathedral, including one for St John's. They would have implemented the new directory in the parish but, given the religious conservatism of Hereford, the old prayer book was probably still used in secret. The three Puritan ministers appointed – William Voyle, George Primrose and William Lowe – 'liv'd in great peace among themselves, and with great unanimity carry'd on the work of the gospel in the city ... till 1660, when they were all cast out.'[73]

All three were in Hereford in 1654, for they appear in the poor law assessments made by the parish overseers, each of them paying five shillings.[74] Educated, sincere and devout though these men were, 'they were apparently uniformly disliked' in this very conservative and royalist city, and the parishioners of St John's were amongst those celebrating King Charles II's restoration in

13

May 1660.[75] The cathedral bell-ringers were paid 10s and the drummers and trumpeters 5s, to make what must have been a very joyful sound.[76]

By the time of the Restoration the parish had a very different population from that of its early days. Gone were the many clerics of the pre-Reformation Catholic period and in their place were members of the Protestant church, although a few recusants still lived in the parish. Whilst the cathedral was not badly damaged during the Civil War, much work was still needed after the Restoration to restore it to its former glory: treasures needed to be returned, windows renewed, furniture, chalices, vestments and other items needed for the seemly conduct of worship restored or replaced. It is not known whether the parish suffered damage to its altar, vestments and so on, but the fact that its life continued during the Interregnum might well have protected it.

As well as the problems in the cathedral, there were problems in the city, for the difficult years of the war had left the citizens of Hereford 'confused and demoralised but ... still showing partiality for cavaliers and papists'.[77] The city was in 'a parlous state, the streets were foul and nastye, with dung and filthy miskins [dunghills or middens] causing more trouble than usual.'[78] But it was not only buildings and streets that showed signs of the damage done by the war – there was also a good deal of poverty in both city and parish. The vicar William Peyton, who followed on from the men appointed during the Interregnum was, like Jonathan Dryden before him, a compassionate man for, in 1662, he had received 'several of the poor into several tenements in the parish of St John without giving good security that this will not harm the parish'. He was to be charged 5s a day if he did not remove them or give assurances that they would not become a charge on the parish.[79]

Whereas previous vicars had reported on recusancy, he was able to report on the conformity of former recusants. In 1670 it was John Prichard. He had been charged with 'contempt of both the church and the Book of Common Prayer but he had now attended church and, it was believed, will now be conformable.'[80] Six years later, it was John Prichot, cooper, and his wife; Edward Floyd and his wife and Frances Simmes and her daughter Elizabeth who had now 'for the space of two years or more been constant frequenters of their parish church'.[81] According to the ecclesiastical census taken that year there were 391 conformists, 2 papists and 16 non-conformists in the parish.[82] It would seem that, at last, in St John's at least, the 'dissemblers and rank papists' had disappeared and that the Protestant reformation had finally arrived.

The 'Glorious Revolution' of 1688 and the accession of the Protestant King William III and his wife Queen Mary caused barely a ripple in the life of the parish.[83] Indeed, the century between the Revolution and the fall of the west end in 1786 was generally a settled one, with no great political or spiritual upheavals. In July 1691, the staunchly Protestant Thomas Gwillim became the vicar of St John's parish. Born in Burghill, on the outskirts of the city and a graduate of Christ Church, Oxford, his family connections placed him firmly amongst 'the worthies of this city and county'. During the Civil War, his great-grandfather had supported the monarchy and the family had lost their lands, although they were returned at the Restoration. However Thomas Gwillim seems to have sloughed off any Royalist connections. He demonstrated his Protestant credentials in 1687, while still the curate at Canon Pyon. Instead of publicly reading James II's Declaration of Indulgence, which attempted to establish greater freedom of religion, 'he tore the hated edict to shreds in the presence of the congregation'.[84] Family worthiness continued after his death in 1768, for one grandson later became mayor of Hereford, whilst a great-grandson held the same office in 1823.

The quiet 18th century

The 18th century was characterised nationally by political controversies between Tories and Whigs which, in Church terms, translated into high and low churchmen. However this did not seem to impact unduly on the parish. Indeed, the early years were marked by an apparent lack of problems so that, when there were visitations, the inspections made by the bishop to the parish, all seemed well. In 1711 the churchwardens reported that 'all things belonging to our parish are in good and sufficient repair as becomes the house of God' and that 'we have examined our books of articles and we find nothing that is presentable to the best of our knowledge.'[85] In 1719 there was nothing to present.[86] However, the parish was adversely affected by the fact that, for many years, both its vicars and their curates presented problems of ill-health or inappropriate behaviour. Perhaps this left little time for religious controversy. These unfortunate appointments might also have been examples of the religious 'stagnation that occurred in the late 17th century and throughout the 18th', a stagnation stemming from the fact that 'there were no suitable provisions for honourable retirement from office'.[87] Instead, if vicars became incapable of performing their duties, they paid a curate out of their own income.

In 1713, William Crowther, a native of Herefordshire, whose father had been the vicar of Tarrington, was appointed as the vicar of St John's. He never actually ministered in his parish, but spent the 53 years of his incumbency in the Droitwich lunatic asylum, dying there in 1766.[88] In 1718, an affidavit sworn by Thomas Amphlett, an apothecary in Droitwich, stated that 'on 25 April 1715 William Crowther, clerk, was brought to his house in Droitwich and put into his care to be cured of a melancholy madness.' There is an interesting, if sad, glimpse into the treatment of the mentally ill at the time, as it went on to say that William Crowther:

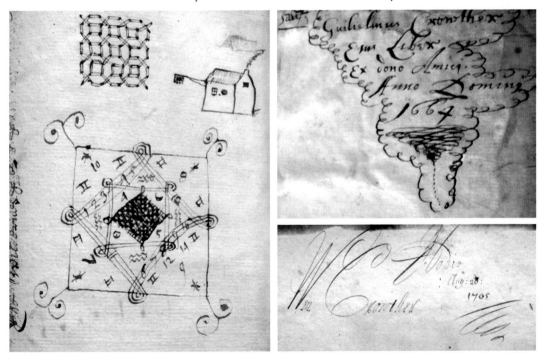

William Crowther's signature (lower right) and a selection of his doodles

was in such a state of melancholy madness that he would have starved himself, to prevent which this deponent with other assistance, was forced to lay him down on the ground upon his back many times to force nourishment into him.[89]

Despite his mental instability, William Crowther was clearly a cultured man, owning a substantial library of books of a religious or philosophical nature, many of which are now in Hereford cathedral library. Before his admission to the asylum, his signature was firm and clear but, as his mental health deteriorated, it became more disordered and eventually his books were covered with illegible scrawls.

Throughout William Crowther's long, but absent, incumbency various curates, members of the vicars choral, were appointed to run the parish and to manage Crowther's financial affairs, but most of them presented problems of ill-health, mental instability or pastoral inadequacy – one suffered from *morbus pediculosis* (lice); another committed suicide. Given the insanity of William Crowther, why quite so many disastrous curates were appointed to the parish is unclear, although the 18th century was one in which eccentric men abounded in the college of the vicars choral.[90] Whatever the reason, this series of unfortunate appointments must have resulted in a very unhappy time for the parishioners. Yet there must still have been a strong commitment to the parish for, in 1760, parishioners commissioned two silver chalices for parish use.[91] These chalices were stolen in 1768 and a reward given for their recovery. It was a generous reward: 'twenty guineas (over and above the forty pounds given by the Act of Parliament on this behalf)'. Presumably somebody decided that the money was worth more than the chalices as they were returned in 1769, but by whom is a mystery.[92]

When William Crowther died in 1766, the parishioners might have hoped for happier times, but the dean and chapter's next appointment was every bit as disastrous. This was Joseph Guest, who spent much of his time as the parish vicar being absent from his duties. A graduate of Worcester College, Oxford, he had been appointed vicar choral in 1754. He held curacies from 1759 before being appointed to the parish. Joseph Guest began well enough and, in 1767, he was involved when the parishioners of St John asked to use the choir, which had recently been grandly refurbished by Bishop Bisse, for their services. They wanted its use for their 'parochial sacraments of the Lords Supper, for their greater decency, as well as for the convenience of the minister and congregation.' Permission was granted *durante bene placito*, upon condition that they paid the two sextons 'the sum of ten shillings yearly for the more than ordinary trouble they will have in cleaning the choir'.[93] This letter, dated August 1772, is an example of the very cap-in-hand situation the parish faced on an annual basis when they had to re-apply for this favour:

St John's chalices

16

we the minister and churchwardens of the parish of St John … beg leave to present our humble thanks to the dean and chapter … for the use of the communion table in the choir of the said church, which with their leave and by their permission only has been from year to year made use of by us and our predecessors … and we now pray that the said dean and chapter will please to continue to use the like favour of for the remainder of this present year on the like terms.[94]

The letter was signed by the parish curate, rather than Joseph Guest since, from 1771 onwards, Guest had become very irregular in both his parochial and choral duties. His name came up at most chapter meetings, with complaints that he had been absent from the choir and neglected his duties.[95] The dean and chapter regularly attempted to get an explanation for his behaviour, but Joseph Guest never explained his absences. Yet, rather than dismiss him, the dean and chapter did all they could to keep him in post. He was even made the 'pricker' for the vicars choral, which involved him in keeping an account of which of the vicars attended services. At least, the dean and chapter must have felt, if he undertook this task, he had to appear for services. This, too, failed to have the desired effect. He was then, in turn, presented to livings at Madley and Holmer but again 'he wholly absented himself from his duties'.[96] Eventually, legal proceedings were taken against him, 'the patience of patrons and creditors being exhausted … in the midst of which he escaped to Bristol, where in 1790 he died, unfriended and unknown, in the 58th year of his age.'[97] The Act book merely noted that 'the defendant is dead'.[98]

In 1782, following the unhappy Joseph Guest's resignation, Richard Underwood, a 'good-humoured easy-going veteran in a scratch wig', was appointed to the parish.[99] He was the most home grown of the St John's vicars, having been born within the parish boundaries on 29 February 1744. Described as one of the 'many eccentric vicars choral', he had a 'mellow tenor voice that greatly helped to revive the spirit of choral service' and was a prominent freemason, a magistrate and a chaplain to the gaol. The parish, it seemed, at last had a competent vicar.[100] In April 1771 he married 'Miss Edwards, daughter of Mr Edwards of Dearndale, an agreeable young lady with £2000 fortune'.[101] Very Jane Austen. Perhaps it is not surprising that in his portrait Richard Underwood looks like a man who enjoyed the pleasures of life. Yet he had a number of disappointments, both professional and personal. Being the bishop's chaplain, he was hopeful that the bishop's patronage would enhance his career for he was:

Richard Underwood in his role as Deputy Provincial Grand Master for Herefordshire in 1805

in great favour in the Palace with fair prospect of future preferment. These hopes, although founded upon actual promises, were not realised, as the bishop's [James Beauclerk] death occurred before an opportunity arose for their fulfilment … but this disappointment was trivial compared with the domestic affliction which soon followed for, in 1789, he lost his amiable wife, a bereavement which he felt severely.

He remarried in 1794, became custos of the vicars choral college and was clearly well-loved and much respected, not least for his 'mildness of disposition, and agreeable manners'. He had 'a vast store of original anecdotes … which his extensive acquaintanceship with the unfortunate inmates of the gaol had furnished and which he narrated in a very amusing and agreeable manner.'[102]

Richard Underwood was in post when, on 17 April 1786, the west front of the cathedral fell. Services began again in June, only two months after the fall, when the parish was given 'the use of the choir for their services during the pleasure of the chapter'.[103] Yet despite these efforts, what was seen as 'the vexed problem of how to deal with the parish of St John' continued to be an issue for the dean and chapter.[104]

Before we consider, in Chapter 3, how this 'vexed issue' was resolved, Chapter 2 will take the story of the parish out of the cathedral and into the parish itself, exploring something of the life of the people living in it.

The west end of the nave after its collapse on 17 April 1786

2   LIFE IN THE PARISH TO THE FALL OF THE WEST END

> Leading events and great personalities make a mark on history … but the everyday affairs of the ordinary man – the merchant, the craftsman, the peasant, the tradesman – leave little record … and if it is difficult to say what the ordinary man was doing, it is even more difficult to say what he was thinking.[1]

The several centuries of parish life before the fall of the west end of the cathedral in 1786 were punctuated by upheavals caused by civil wars, plague and epidemic, a religious Reformation and a decapitated king. Although hundreds of people appear in the available archives, often little more than a name comes down through the centuries and, where records do still exist, they comment mainly on the rogues and the rebels, rather than the ordinary man or woman. However records, such as parish registers, although telling us nothing about the everyday affairs of the ordinary man, give glimpses into major life events, such as birth, marriage and death; whilst the city records, known as the 'Sack books', give a little information about the rogues, and about how the city and parish dealt with poverty and what we would now call health and safety issues.

Hereford Cathedral's Norman font (photo courtesy of Malcolm Thurlby)

Births, Marriages and Burials

In 1538 parishes were ordered to keep registers of births, marriages and deaths, but those for St John only survive from 1604, and, as there is rarely any information with which to flesh out a story, only glimpses of the thousands of parish births, marriages and deaths can be included here. At the beginning of his parishioners' lives, the vicar of St John's would have been responsible for baptising newly born babies in the font that still stands in the cathedral today. The Elizabethan prayer book instructed priests to 'admonish the people that they defer not the baptism of infants any longer than the Sunday or holy day after the child be born, unless upon a great and reasonable cause declared to the curate and by him approved.'[2] One example of this rapid baptism was that of John, the son of John Lodges and his wife Joan, who was born on 'Thursday 16 December at 6 in the morning and baptised the same day 1671.'[3]

Although both parents were named in the parish registers, it was the father who would, with family and friends, bring the new born baby to the church as a woman was not allowed back into the church after childbirth until she had been 'churched' or purified after the birth of her child. At the church door, the baptismal party was greeted by the priest. He would bless the baby, put salt into its mouth as a symbol of the reception of wisdom and then, having exorcised any demons, would take the baptismal party to the font for the anointing and baptism. A chrism cloth would be placed on the baby's head, to stop the consecrated oil from accidentally rubbing off.

Baptism would normally be a joyful occasion signalling new life but often, at a time when life expectancy was short, life and death went hand in hand, with the stark entries in the parish registers reflecting the sadness of such events. On 15 January 1611, James Davies and John his son were both buried; ten days later another son, James, was buried.[4] Even 400 years later, it is still possible to imagine the grief of a wife who lost both her husband and two children within weeks of each other. Causes of death were not given, but they might well have died from the plague which was endemic at the time. Death in childbirth was also common. In 1628, John Jones, a clerk in holy orders, buried his wife Eleanor and baptised his new daughter on the same day.[5] Any joy he would have had in the new baby must have been overshadowed by grief about his wife, as well as anxiety about how to care for his new child.

There are, not surprisingly, numerous clerical baptisms as, by the time parish registers began, strictures against clerical marriage had been lifted. Where a profession is given, it shows a parish in which there were only a handful of baptisms for the children of professional men; most are for working men and women. Occasionally the father was a soldier. In 1715, the year of the first Jacobite uprising, two soldiers, William Tomkins and Thomas Cox, both had children baptised.[6] Nothing is known of their regiments, but it is easy to imagine that they were having some leave in their homes in the parish before setting out again for war. Anxiety about their futures could perhaps be forgotten for a short time, whilst they celebrated new

The uniform of the 15th Regiment of Foot in 1750

life with feasting and merriment. The same must have applied, some fifty years later, to John Andrews and his wife. John Andrews was with the 15th Regiment of Foot, a regiment that was sent in 1776 to North Carolina to fight in the American Revolutionary War.[7] The baptism, in the same year, of their daughter Lydia, might well have occurred just before her father left the parish to fight in America, leaving an anxious wife at home with her new baby.

There was even the occasional adult baptism. In April 1693 Francis Williams, a 'black servant to Mr James Walwyn', a merchant trading in Barbados, was baptised.[8] At that time, bringing a black slave back from their plantations was becoming popular with slave owners. Such slaves, working as butlers, footmen and so on, were intended as another piece of exotica belonging to the affluent families in which they found themselves. Life for Francis Williams was probably hard. He might well have been lonely and possibly the only black person in the parish or, indeed, in Hereford, but it would have been infinitely preferable to life as a slave on his master's plantation. He might indeed have felt himself to be a fortunate man.

Another curious adult baptism took place in 1720, when 'Amos Rogers, born of Anabaptist parents, and aged about eight and forty years', was baptised.[9] Anabaptists, who believed in adult baptism, were members of one of the many radical groups which arose on the continent during the Protestant Reformation. Dutch and Flemish Anabaptists who fled from persecution on the continent might find themselves executed or burnt at the stake in England. By the 18th century 'the name had become one of abuse with evil associations and was largely repudiated'.[10] Perhaps Amos had found himself being abused or persecuted for his beliefs and had decided to join the more mainstream Anglican congregation in his parish.

Although most of the baptisms in the registers are for legitimate children, 'base' or 'unlawfully begotten' children were not overlooked. Usually it was the mother who was named in the register but, on one occasion, it was the father who was left literally holding the baby. When Elizabeth, the 'supposed daughter' of William Thomas, 'ffeltmaker', was baptised in 1633, the mother's name was not given.[11]

Pre-Reformation marriages also began in the church porch, rather than at the altar, with a nuptial mass and a blessing in the church after the couple had exchanged vows. These solemn events would be crowned with 'eating, drinking, dancing, music, jesting and sexual innuendo', not all of it after the event, with the members of the wedding party often arriving in a mildly intoxicated state.[12] The earliest entries for parish marriages are two in Bishop Mayew's register in the early years of Henry VIII's reign, when he was still happily married to Katherine of Aragon and hopeful of a male heir to the throne. In 1513, the vicar of St John's married Richard Mydroffe of St Martin's parish to Margery Wynstanley of St John's. In 1516 he married John Combe of Whitbourne, a village on the Herefordshire border, to Elizabeth Dyke of St John's parish.[13] Nothing else is known about these two couples but, with a little imagination, it is easy to see them, dressed in their best outfits, being blessed at the parish altar in a cathedral which would have been bright with painted frescoes and stained glass.

More than two hundred years later, in 1775, an unusual wedding occurred when 'Thomas Clark and Mary Smith, both confined to the House of Correction in the City of Hereford, were married in the church of St John.'[14] As they were illiterate, both signed the register with 'X' rather than a signature.[15] In the 18th century the House of Correction or Bridewell was a place of fascination for the polite society of Hereford, who would come to stare at the 'vagrants and other idle and disorderly persons housed there' being put on view by their gaolers. It also

The House of Correction in the early 18th century (Thomas Symonds)

housed the 'deserving poor' and perhaps Thomas and Mary were amongst this group, hoping to find a way out of the penury of life there. It must have been a terrible place – some years earlier, the keeper was sacked for neglecting the residents who 'were like to starve for want of care'.[16]

Unlike baptisms and marriages, burials would have been sadder and more sombre affairs but there would still have been much conviviality after the funeral service.[17] Only the rich could afford coffins. The poorer members of the parish would be transported to the parish altar on a cart or a bier. It is possible that the parish would have had a communal coffin, a wooden box used during the funeral service, before the burial of the deceased, with the body being wrapped in a winding sheet, since no-one, not even a pauper, would be buried without a shroud. Even these were subject to political intervention. Between 1666 and 1680, Acts of Parliament were passed requiring everyone, other than plague victims and the destitute, to be buried in woollen, rather than linen, shrouds. The reason for this was an economic one as the woollen trade, which contributed much to the wealth and prosperity of the country, was under threat from new materials and foreign imports. William Peyton, the vicar of St John's between 1635 and 1679, was one of those from the parish who conformed, as he is listed as having been buried in wool. Those who refused to obey this law had to pay a penalty but wealthier members of society 'could afford to factor the fine for funeral clothes of a more high status design into their costs'.[18] One such in the parish was Herbert Tryst, Esq., whose wife Matilda was, in 1726, 'buried in linen and the penalty paid to the poor of the parish'.[19]

At the other end of the social scale, when the servant of William Davis was buried in 1610 'being drowned in the Wye the week before', he was unnamed, with only his master's name being given.[20] One of the saddest of the burial entries was for Francis Aylestone (a child found at Aylestone) who was baptised 10 January 1726 and buried 23 January 1726.[21] Sometimes burials resulted after parishioners had met with unusual ends. In 1731 Benjamin Edwin died after falling out of a window in Broad Street; a year later Nicholas Philpot died after discharging a pistol at his head; in 1735 Richard Mills died from a visitation of God in a pigsty in the parish. A visitation of God was a phrase used for what we might now call death by natural causes.[22]

There were also burials after murders had taken place. On 20 October 1607 David Gwyn was buried, and on the following day William Williams, 'being slain both of them in Haywood on the same day'.[23] Haywood was a royal forest in the early Middle Ages, having been, in 1141, granted to Miles of Gloucester by the Empress Matilda when she made him earl of Hereford. It was a very rural parish without any sizeable settlements and quite why these two men were murdered there is a mystery. Some years later, in 1634, another murder occurred, this time in the cathedral precincts when John Traherne was stabbed with a rapier, dying instantly from a deep wound. A witness was at the 'shoppe of one John Hughes, weaver being near the cathedral church', when he heard a noise in the street. He rushed out of the shop to find the dead man and, standing over him, William Sergeant, who admitted that he was the murderer.[24] What happened next is not recorded but, although this might well have been a random killing, given the tensions at the time between King and Parliament, Catholics and Protestants, it could equally well have been a politically or religiously motivated one. This was, after all, the period in which many Puritans were leaving England for New England in America in order to escape religious persecution.

Finally there were the oddities. In 1605, Gerram Powell, 'one of Mr Harley's strollers' was buried.[25] Nothing is known about either him or Mr Harley, although travelling players were a regular feature of life in Tudor England. It is easy to imagine a troupe coming to Hereford in 1605 and performing their plays in the city and then Gerram being taken ill and dying in the parish.

What did people do?

As for jobs, parish and other registers rarely give occupations but, where they do, it helps to show a social mix, which ranged from a handful of gentry and professional people living mainly in Castle Street, to paupers and servants in Gwynne Street. Even after the Reformation, when there would have been far fewer clergy serving the cathedral, clerics in the parish were still numerous. The records for parish recusants provide glimpses into trades before the parish registers were started. In the 1590s there were several trades connected with animal skins, such as a shoemaker, a saddler and several glovers. Alice Cooke was an apple seller; there were butchers and a boatman. Parish records show that professional men were scarce, with only two 'doctors in physick' and two surgeons. Although 'gents' do appear, in the main the jobs were those of working, rather than professional, men, such as bakers, barbers, carpenters, cobblers, joiners, labourers, locksmiths, masons, mercers, painters, servants, tailors and weavers. As the Wye, a working river, ran through the parish, bargemen and watermen, not surprisingly, also appear, but Thomas Davies, a seafaring man, was a long way from any coast. There were sometimes more unusual jobs: an armourer in 1634,[26] a serjeant at law in 1687, a book seller and watchmaker in 1704,[27] a brief-gatherer and a sword bearer in 1717, a peruke (wig) maker in 1758,[28] an excise officer in 1768 and a comedian, Thomas Catton, in 1784.[29]

Pleasure, Punishment and Public Order

Life must have been hard for these generally poor parishioners, especially as many pleasurable recreations, such as gambling and card playing, were frowned on, with injunctions against such behaviour going back before the Reformation. In 1530, two deacons and two sub-deacons from the cathedral were discovered by the mayor of Hereford playing cards at night in the house of one John Coke of St John's parish. They were told to attend all services for a week, ranging from Matins, held during the night, through to Compline, the night prayer made before retiring.[30] After the Reformation, 'unlawful games', including bear and bull baiting, bowling, as well as 'dancing on the Lord's day' continued to be prohibited.[31]

A picture of early Morris Dancers: a piper, hobby-horse, Maid Marian, Robin and a jester

However, times did change and, in 1633, Charles I issued the *Declaration on Lawful Sports*, based on an edict first set out in 1618 by his father about recreation on Sundays. James I had been disturbed to find that his 'subjects were debarred from lawful recreations upon Sundays after evening prayers and on holy-days'. He prudently considered that his subjects, who laboured hard all the week, needed recreations to refresh their spirits. He made a list of those recreations which were allowed on Sundays and those which were not. Dancing for men and women, archery for men, leaping, vaulting, may-poles and Morris dances were all allowed. Women were allowed to carry rushes to church in order to decorate it. Yet some pleasures were still barred and the city records have frequent references to people being indicted for allowing unlawful gaming. One such, in 1635, was John Richards of Broad Street who had allowed shuffleboard on Sundays.[32]

However, despite being allowed various kinds of recreation, people still misbehaved, committed offences and broke various laws. Brawling seems to have been more common then, fortunately, than it is now. In 1520, William Hill, sergeant of the king's mace, 'distrained a carpet and pewter pot, within the vicarage of St John's ... for certain indictments.'[33] Along came Nicholas Walwyn, a cathedral canon, who 'pulled the sergeant by his head'. Uproar then ensued between church and city dignitaries, a not uncommon event in the history of town and church relations. It was, however, amicably resolved when Nicholas Walwyn agreed to pay the aggrieved sergeant 6s 8d and to meet him in the cathedral where they took each 'other by the hands ... for a sign and token of love between the church and city'. They then repaired to Goldsmith's tavern, 'as lovers and friends arm in arm ... and the canons of the chapter there gave wine to the mayor and others to the value of 20 pence.'[34]

Drunkenness was also common and Cabbage Lane, today's very smart Church Street, was often the scene of anti-social behaviour. In 1628, Isaac Clark of Bromyard was found drunk in Cabbage Lane and behaving 'rudely, barbarously and uncivilly … uttering the most blasphemous and horrible oaths viz. god's blood and god's wounds.'[35] Several years later, John Holt a glover, followed John and Mary Cutler up Cabbage Lane, calling her 'a filthy sot and the spawn of a bastard' and him 'a knave' and shouting that he 'did not care a fart or a turd for him nor for any man in England.' John Holt, it seemed, was 'often times drunk' and, when in that state, he scolded and railed in a most unchristian manner to his neighbours. Holt was ordered to keep the peace.[36]

People were also charged with slander. In 1705, Eliza Thorp, 'an honest civil woman and a widow' was, involved in a 'great tumult' when Richard Griffiths of St John's 'in a very rude and passionate manner … told her she was the devil's whore several times'. Justice, it seems, was done when Eliza was awarded a bill of expenses amounting to £4 10s 6d.[37] Some forty years later, Lucy Jones, spinster of the parish, won her case against a butcher, Herbert Lane, who had called her 'a strumpet and a whore'.[38] A glimpse into what must have been a warm summer's evening in the parish occurred in yet another case of defamation when Magdalen Savaker, aged about 71, was 'sitting within the door of her dwelling … in the evening with the door opened, when the defendant came to the door with only his shirt on.' However, it was not to remain a peaceful scene, as accusations and counter-accusations of whoring flew about.[39]

Theft was another concern of the city fathers. A glimpse of Pipe Lane (Gwynne Street), said to be the birthplace of Nell Gwynne, occurs when 'Jane Hayward was charged with stealing sheets which were hanging on a hedge in Pipe Lane in the garden of Thomas Duppa gent.'[40] The same Thomas Duppa also found himself in trouble some years later, for he clearly did not have the Georgian equivalent of planning permission when he set up posts and railings to enclose his garden. He was fined fourscore and five pounds and instructed to take them down. He clearly ignored this injunction, for a year later he was fined again.[41] The outcomes of delinquency in terms of punishment are rarely given but one punishment was to be whipped in the market place and then to stand in the pillory, with the offence for which the punishment was being meted out written on a board in capital letters.[42] In 1658, Elizabeth Pews, who had stolen a pair of grey stockings, suffered this punishment when she was stripped to her waist and whipped until she bled.[43]

The city records for the Tudor and early Stuart period are full of what we would now call social, environmental and health and safety issues. The authorities were at pains to keep the streets clean and the people honest. Visitors to the city were charged to leave their weapons in their inn; the price to be charged by bakers, brewers, butchers, chandlers and tanners was fixed; parishioners were fined for keeping dunghills, faggots, and middens outside their back doors; swans and ducks were not allowed to be at large; people were not allowed to be abroad after 9pm unless they were of good name and had some form of light with them.[44] Things were not much different during the Commonwealth: in 1656, the parishioners were reprimanded about the state of their streets which were 'very foul and nasty for want of scavengers to keep them as clean and wholesome as in other cities'. They were told to appoint scavengers who would keep the streets clean on a weekly basis.[45] By the time that Charles II was monarch, people were forbidden to throw the contents of their chamber pots out of the windows.[46]

There were frequent complaints that the pumps in the parish were not being kept in good repair. This seems odd for, in the days before one could simply turn on a tap, having a supply of fresh water from the local pump would have been essential. The pump would also have been crucial when a fire occurred, as must have happened quite often in the days when buildings were mostly of wood and candles were the only source of light. What was the widow Lynke thinking when, in 1663, she made 'a fire within a little shop in narrow Cabbage Lane, being very low built and having no chimney within it, whereby there have been several accidents like to happen by the said fire prejudicial and dangerous to the whole city'?[47]

People also feared competition in trade, seeking to protect the interests of local people and to remove those whom they saw as outsiders. In 1628, the guild of tailors complained about people coming into the city and practising their handicraft, to the 'great hindrance and prejudice' of those already established. As a result of this competition, those tailors already established in the city fell into poverty and sickness. The mayor agreed that the incomers should be conveyed out of the city; the two miscreants in the parish, Nicholas Oates, his wife and children and Francis Jones, his wife and children would have been included in this decree.[48]

Poverty and Parish Relief

A recurring theme throughout this whole period was the question of how to deal with the poor, with the origins of the Poor Law system dating back to the late medieval period. Although begging was prohibited by Edward VI, in 1555, in the reign of Queen Mary, a list was prepared of the poor people of the city, who were to be granted sufficient licence to allow them to 'go abroad to beg, get and receive the charitable alms of the inhabitants of the county of Hereford'.[49] In St John's parish, there were eight such people: John Morris and his wife, James Kerry, Elizabeth Hodson, Lawrence Gawens, his wife and daughter and Elianor Borsley. Such leniency was not to last for, in 1572, the Vagabonds Act called for unlicensed vagabonds to be whipped and a hole burned through the gristle of the right ear. In 1597 the Act for the relief of the poor created the role of overseers, charged with setting the poor rate for a parish, and then collecting and distributing it. In 1601 what has become known as the old Poor Law Act was passed, formalising existing legislation with parishes being made responsible for providing outdoor relief, such as clothing and food; indoor relief in alms-houses for the 'deserving' poor, the elderly and those with a disability; and workhouses for the 'undeserving', those who refused to work.[50]

Concern for the provision of poor relief carried on from monarch to monarch. In 1612, when James I had followed Elizabeth's long reign, the city worthies had to ensure that 'rogues and vagabonds were taken to the house of correction, that the poor, lame and impotent were given relief, that strangers who were harboured be sent back to the place of their last abode and landlords punished.'[51]

Much of the Civil War uproar in the city would have been centred on the castle and the cathedral, both of which were in the parish. Quite how tense life in the parish would have been is impossible to know but many of those who were prominent in the city during the Civil War, both Royalists and Parliamentarians, lived cheek by jowl in the parish streets. Poor relief contributions did not discriminate between Royalists and Parliamentarians, for a 1654 list still exists of their contributions to the poor rate. The list was headed by those contributing ten shillings and began with the Parliamentarians Major Wroth Rogers and Thomas Rawlins, with the third named being James Rodd, a former mayor and staunch Royalist.[52]

Although poor relief would have been given regularly to most of those needing it, the parish overseers who dispensed the money paid into the poor law coffers had, it seems, their own prejudices. In a small but diverse parish such as St John's, they would probably have known all those applying. They did not, it appears, look kindly on the more Royalist members of the parish. Margaret Berrington was the widow of Ottwell Berrington, a gunsmith and 'a faithful subject of his late majesty of most famous memory'. From 1654 onwards she appears regularly in the records, claiming that her allowance was often withheld by the parish overseers, James Tudor and William Bosworth, 'being covetous persons for their own ends'.[53] Things did not seem to improve after the restoration of the monarchy for, in 1661, by which time, aged '70, impotent, lame and her sight failing her', she complained that she had been 'most unconsciously cruelly and uncharitably dealt with by one John Harper, corviser [a shoemaker], one of the overseers' who had, it seemed, withheld her money for half a year, forcing her to sell all her goods to 'buy bread & faggots to preserve her from starving or perishing'.[54] What happened is not recorded, but Margaret was not alone in having such problems. Another petitioner in the same year was William Hatfort who, 'being aged & lame of his limbs, not being able to dress himself & also very imperfect of his sight fearing, he shall be dark he not being able to help himself in anything', pleaded with the magistrates for his allowance which had been withheld by the old overseers for nine weeks and by the new for six.[55] It is tempting to wonder whether he too was discriminated against because of Royalist sympathies.

However, charity did get dispensed to at least some of those in need. In 1662, Thomas Mason, aged about 100, born within the parish and with a poor aged wife, sought help from the overseers on the grounds that 'his labour was spent, and he was in a distressed condition, helpless and comfortless and likely to perish for want of succour.' He was granted 1s weekly.[56] In the same year, John Thomas also sought financial help. He had probably suffered a stroke for he had been 'struck in a strange manner and in a miserable condition not able to move ... and all his one side quite dead.' His wife had worn herself out trying to care for him, and in 'turning and winding' him. He was granted 2s 6d a week.[57]

In 1666, the parish was ordered to pay 6d a week to Henry Traherne, being 'a poor old man ... aged above fourscore years ... his limbs being stupefied, he was not able any longer to work for his living having no estate or means to maintain himself.' He had inhabited an old barn in the parish for about 12 years and also requested a place in an almshouse as soon as there was a vacancy. Mary Williams, however, much preferred her own home.[58] She was a 'poor widow being deaf ... with nine fatherless children ... through tempestuous wind and stormy weather part of her poor habitation had been destroyed, unthatched, and blown down, with the chimney also much in hazard to fall.' She was granted 2s a week from the parish, which allowed her to both feed her children and 'rectify her poor cottage destroyed by the late winds.'[59] Another sad case in the same year concerned a wife with a spendthrift husband. Jane Harris's dead husband Simon, through his 'ill courses and extravagancy' had left her and her two children (plus a third expected) in a 'very sad and deplorable condition, being now friendless and harbourless, and knows not where to go for succour.' When her husband was alive she had managed to look after her family out of the money she could save from her husband and from her own industry, but on her own she had fallen on hard times.[60]

Another woman who was left with a fatherless child was the daughter of Thomas Price. This was the story of a married man having an affair, for William Morgan had used 'dulcet smooth terms' to seduce the daughter of an aged shepherd. Not only did she have a 'bastard child' now about five years, but the said daughter had also lost her sight. Thomas Price, the shepherd, together with his other two daughters, had tried to support the whole family but 'being no longer able so to do', he asked that the good worships would be 'pleased … to take a speedy course … for some certain maintenance for the relief and succour of his bastard child begotten on your poore petitioners blind daughter.'[61]

Most of the disputes about poor law payments came from the petitioners for charity but one came from those assessed to pay their dues. In 1686, those canons whose homes were in the parish felt that they should not have to pay their poor law dues, on the grounds that their houses were extra-parochial. Although this was disputed by the parish overseers, their objection was respected for a while until an unusual incident occurred when:

> a new-born infant in a bundle of clothes was attached to the knocker of a house in Canon Row and found there by a servant. The canon in residence, unwilling to accept the unexpected gift, sent it to the overseer, and so recognised his relations to the parish which had hitherto been disputed.[62]

As well as relieving poverty through the poor law assessments, some of the poor relief came from the parish's charitable bequests. In May 1680, John Walters established a charity which was to bear his name until well into the 20th century. It was established 'out of the love and affection he did bear towards the parish of Saint John, being the place of his nativity'. At a later date, his widow Alice Walters 'out of the love and affection she did bear towards her husband' confirmed that the rents from various properties they owned should be used to fund the charity. The trustees of the charity, the churchwardens of the parish, were to 'nominate and appoint seven poor decayed widows of the parish of good name and repute (but not non-conformists) they think to be the fitter object of their charity.'[63] These decayed widows were to receive, each Sunday, after divine service, a two penny loaf of bread. They also received 'every feast day of the nativity and Easter day, Whitsunday and All Saints day a four penny loaf'. The widows had to be 'conformable to the liturgy, discipline and doctrine' of the Anglican Church and regularly attend the parish church for divine service; they also had to avoid being 'a common swearer, drunkard or disturber of the peace'. If they broke any of these strictures, their charity was withdrawn and if they didn't mend their ways within a month they were rejected for ever. Whilst the accounts consist mainly of the figures relating to the charity, there is an occasional 'human' story. In 1759 widow Owen 'refused to accept her loaves'. It is easy to imagine an independent woman who turned up her nose, saying 'you can keep your charity, I don't want it'.

After these glimpses of parish life before the fall of the west end, Chapter 3 continues the history of the parish 'altar', a history that takes the parish into its heyday in the Victorian era.

3 FROM THE FALL OF THE WEST END TO THE DISSOLUTION OF THE PARISH

The later 19th century was a high point for the parochial history of St John's. Sufficient of its parish records survive for us to see it functioning in a very real sense as a parish.[1]

1786 to Queen Victoria's accession in 1837

By the time of the dramatic fall of the cathedral's west end, the parish would have had a very different population from that of its early days. Gone were the many priests of the pre-Reformation period and in their place were shopkeepers, labourers and artisans and, in the smarter streets, a few professional people. Many of these residents felt a strong sense of belonging to 'their' parish church and, particularly in the Victorian period, were fiercely loyal to it.

After the upheavals of 1786, the parishioners and their vicar, Richard Underwood, enjoyed a few peaceful years, happily using the choir for their services. It was not, however, to last, for by 1790 the burial of the city dead had become a real problem. A letter was sent by the dean and chapter to all the city parishes, expressing concern about the overcrowded state of the cathedral churchyard. As a result, it was decreed that from 25 March 1791 only those who died within the cathedral precincts could be buried there.[2]

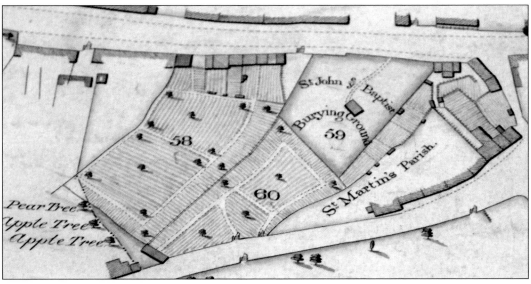

The tithe map of 1840 showing St John's burial ground at Blackmarston

The parish burial records immediately reflected this, with burials dropping from an average of 18 a year to just one or two and, in 1795, none. Parishes were forced to open their own burial ground, with the one for St John's being about half a mile from the Close at Blackmarston, one of the parish's outlying districts.[3]

Another problem came hot on the heels of that of the burial ground, for, in 1794, the dean and chapter requested that the parish altar be moved from the choir to the north transept. The parishioners objected to this on the grounds of inconvenience and cost, and the dean and chapter Act book has a number of entries in which tetchiness and irritation emanate from both sides. After the cost of repairing the damaged west end, the dean and chapter complained about the additional expense of moving and furnishing the parish 'church', while the parishioners felt slighted and undervalued. However, in 1796, tempers were eventually smoothed, with the dean and chapter Act book having the briefest of comments that 'the north transept be opened for service on Sunday 19th June'.[4] Not everyone approved of this move. Some considered that the north transept had been 'most lamentably disfigured by numerous pews and seats, appropriated to the parishioners of St John',[5] with the box pews that were provided being 'crammed together like cattle pens'.[6] If, as suggested earlier, the parish altar was in the north transept at its foundation some six centuries earlier, then its place in the cathedral had, after many centuries, come full circle.

The north transept with its pews viewed looking south

Richard Underwood, who had been the vicar throughout all these changes, died in 1819 and was succeeded by James Garbett. When, as an undergraduate, he went to Christ Church, Oxford, his father was described in the university register as a 'plebeian', a category for parents who were not noblemen, gentlemen or clerks in holy orders. Humble though his background was, four of his six sons were educated, first at Hereford Cathedral School, and then, with scholarships, at Brasenose College.[7] His eldest son, James, was a clergyman and theo-

James Garbett

logian, as well as being elected professor of poetry at Oxford; and one of his grandsons, Cyril Garbett, became archbishop of York.[8]

On becoming vicar, James Garbett quickly became involved in the further beautifying of the north transept, with a new gallery being erected and extra seating provided.[9] However, cathedral services were still clashing with those of the parish and, in 1834, 'several respectable inhabitants of the parish' petitioned Dean Merewether for their own church. Various sites were suggested, meetings were held, and committees set up, but, over a long number of years, nothing ever came of this suggestion.[10] James Garbett was clearly a popular and much loved priest and, when he left St John's in 1840, his parishioners presented him with some silver plate, with the hope that it would be 'a memorial of our gratitude for your long continued exertions in this parish'. In response James Garbett said that he had:

> had the happiness to preside over the spiritual interests of St John's for 22 years. During that period, I have experienced, in connection with the discharge of my ministerial duties many joys and many sorrows; I have had much to comfort and much to harass me; much to discourage, and much to animate. I have lived amongst you contented and happy. I should be sadly wanting were I capable of quitting the field of ministerial labours without a sigh, without a tear, without many painful feelings of regret.[11]

The Victorian Era

The appointment of John Hanbury, who became the next vicar of the parish, coincided with the start of the Victorian period and the heyday of the parish. Little is known about him, probably because he was a good, respectable vicar who worked hard in his parish. His name appeared regularly in the local newspapers as a subscriber to and supporter of various worthy institutions. For example, very early in his incumbency, he gave 12 volumes of the *Lives of Church Reformers* and Addison's *Evidence of Christianity* to the Hereford Mechanics Institute.[12] He seems to have been a serious man, although, at a meeting called to arrange Hereford's festivities on the occasion of the Princess Royal's wedding, he proposed that the juveniles, on whose behalf he appeared, should be given a 'glass of wine, a bun, and a new sixpence'.[13] Perhaps there was something of the frivolous in him after all.

Hanbury's arrival occurred shortly before the start of several years of major restoration work on the cathedral, work which was disruptive to both the cathedral and the parish. Not surprisingly therefore, early in Hanbury's incumbency, the question of building a separate parish church was raised yet again. In 1844, the bishop, Thomas Musgrave, chaired a meeting of the Diocesan Church Building Society, at which he showed plans for a proposed new church which he thought could be built without 'troubling the parishioners, except in the way of voluntary contributions'. The stone was to come 'without charge' from the quarry belonging to the dean

John Hanbury

31

and chapter at Capler.[14] An interesting comment at this meeting was that 'the right of the parishioners to a portion of the cathedral for divine worship is by no means clearly defined, and it is somewhat remarkable that they have, at various times, been moved about to different parts of the sacred fabric.'[15]

Nothing came of this proposal and, by November 1848, the parishioners had had enough of being side-lined during the restorations taking place in the cathedral. They sent a lengthy letter of complaint to Dean Merewether and the chapter, the gist of it being that, although the parish consisted of about 1,300 people, ever since the cathedral restoration had started there had been nowhere for them to worship. They were incensed because the 'gallery, wooden floor and pews in the north transept' where they had worshipped had 'been altogether removed and taken away but by whose sanction and authority we know not, and the pews may now be seen as forming part of the wooden hoarding surrounding the cathedral.'[16] The parishioners demanded that the floor and pews be replaced and that suitable accommodation be found for their worship, either in the cathedral or elsewhere. A year later, the Act book still talked of the need to resolve the 'want of accommodation occasioned by the exclusion of the inhabitants from the cathedral'.[17] There is something a little puzzling and perhaps almost petulant about these grumbles as, according to an 1851 trade directory, services for the parish were, during the alterations, being performed in the nave.[18] Displaced they might have been, but their worship was still able to continue. Yet still nothing happened and two years later Dean Merewether died, without any resolution of the parishioners' demands.

Dean Merewether was succeeded by Richard Dawes and serious consideration was again given to building a separate parish church, with matters dragging on in an unsatisfactory manner for several more years. Eventually, in 1854, John Hanbury complained of the 'great dissatisfaction of his parishioners at their not having any place of worship', suggesting the Lady Chapel, rather than a new building, as a suitable place.[19] Heels were dragged yet again. Five years later the dean and chapter said that they still were 'not in a position to make any definite arrangement [about the use of the Lady Chapel as the parish church] until further progress has been made towards the restoration of the cathedral.'[20] This vexed question of whether there should be a separate parish church rumbled on for several more years, with a letter in the *Hereford Times* in January 1860 reading as follows:

> after the thousands of pounds which have been spent to clear out the many deformities which time and taste had accumulated within the walls of our venerable cathedral, can it be true that the authorities intend choking up the elegant Lady Chapel as a church for St John's parish – I can scarcely believe that the body of gentlemen who have made such noble efforts to make our cathedral what it is would, for a moment, permit it ... I cannot believe the parishioners wish it. If a church must be had for St John's parish close at hand, why not purchase the Globe Inn [in Broad Street] and build on that site, with a gothic archway beneath an organ gallery for access to the cathedral close, signed, *a churchman*. [21]

It was during these battles about a separate parish church that, on the death of John Hanbury in 1860, the high churchman John Goss became the vicar, remaining in post until his death in 1877. He came from a musical family, being the son of the composer Sir John Goss, thought by some to be one of the most important early Victorian composers. During his career, John Goss senior was the organist at St Paul's and then, from 1856, composer to the Chapel Royal.[22]

He was a man with a 'gentle and ineffectual manner', whereas his son 'undoubtedly had a very keen taste for buckling on his armour and descending into the field of battle'.[23] As soon as he was appointed, John Goss had to enter the fray, both about the merits of a separate church and about what had again become a pressing problem, the burial of the dead.

One of the first tasks for the newly appointed John Goss was to inform the dean and chapter that the burial ground of St John's at Blackmarston 'was all but full', and that he proposed to accept the offer of land made by Bishop Renn Hampden for a city burial ground near the current crematorium site in which each parish would have a section. This was opened in 1863 and three years later the Blackmarston burial ground was levelled and closed to all but people having family vaults there.[24]

As for a separate parish church, all ideas for an alternative place of worship continued to be ignored and eventually quashed. In 1861, Gilbert Scott, who was responsible for the restoration of the cathedral, argued that the fitting up of the Lady Chapel, rather than the building of a separate church for the parish, was now of 'pressing importance'.[25] Yet, it was not until October 1863, a few months after the cathedral had been re-opened after years of restoration, that the dean and chapter agreed to grant 'to the parishioners of St John the free use of the Lady Chapel for parochial purposes'.

Money still had to be raised to make this a reality and a committee was formed to raise £300 for 'the necessary fittings [including a small organ] for the celebration of Divine service'. Clearly, the parish was still a poor one, for services were 'largely attended by the poorer class of parishioners'.[26] Two years later, in 1865, some thirty years after the issue of a separate place for parish worship was first mooted, there was a grand celebration when the Lady Chapel was

Hereford Cathedral c.1860

opened as the parish church. It was a 'brilliantly fine day', with a huge crowd gathering where the 'soft beauty of the cathedral Close, the renovated stateliness of the cathedral, the play of light and shade upon buttress, pinnacle, and turret all formed a beautiful picture, set in a rich frame of foliage formed by the magnificent elms'.[27] Such journalism may seem a touch hyperbolic, but it does conjure up something of a paradise in the centre of Hereford. It was abundantly clear that the parishioners of St John wanted their own 'church' inside the cathedral. They clearly valued it, as can be judged not only from the increasing parish congregation but also from the way in which furnishings continued to be installed to beautify it.

A year later, it was reported that, 'in consequence of the increase in the Sunday afternoon congregation, it was necessary to provide 60 additional seats, making upwards of 300 in all, freely open to rich and poor alike.'[28] The diocesan calendar also provided an enthusiastic report on the newly opened 'church', saying that the Lady Chapel now had:

> new oaken seats for the clergy and choir; a new altar table of the same wood, with carvings, and an elaborately worked super-frontal altar cloth of a crimson colour. The preacher, instead of delivering his discourse from an old chair reversed and covered with baize, now occupies a handsome looking pulpit ... the sittings, too, are all new ... the vicar, besides contributing liberally to the fund, presented the hangings ... the churchwardens gave a brass reading desk and a pair of candlesticks.

However, a suggestion of the tensions between the parish and the dean and chapter that often simmered below the surface appeared again with the final comment that 'it is with much regret that we have to state that the only entrance the parishioners have to their beautiful parish church, is through a rough wooden gate of the meanest description, the remedy being entirely in the hands of the dean and chapter.'[29]

John Goss was not an easy man as far as the dean and chapter were concerned and with his high church leanings he had clashes with them both about his clerical dress and the men he invited to give sermons. At the time he was parish vicar, there was a move amongst some of the clergy towards the greater use of 'vestments and customs which most people thought had gone for ever at the Reformation ... priests began to appear in chasubles or copes, and to introduce into the services such things as tapers and incense.'[30] John Goss, like other clergy, was an enthusiast for such change and some of them must have appeared in this more flamboyant clerical gear. They were soon reprimanded by the bishop and, in 1869, he instructed those cathedral clergy who wore a 'stole or a scarf that it be of plain black without golden fringe or cross'.[31] Three years later there were still some who did not obey this stricture, and, when members of the cathedral body were told that they must conform to the canonical dress of the cathedral, 'that is to say, long surplices, reaching to within four or five inches of the ground ... stoles or scarves of plain black without golden or coloured fringe, cross or other ornament', it was specifically 'ordered that John Goss be informed of this ruling'.[32]

In 1870, theological controversy raged (albeit politely) when John Goss was forced by the dean and chapter to cancel a sermon due to be given by the Reverend Luke Rivington, the superior of the Society of the Holy Ghost. A letter of reprimand was sent to John Goss by the dean and chapter, (after the sermon had been cancelled), in which he was told that to have such a person preaching would have:

caused great scandal in the city of Hereford … as it was to take place in that part of the cathedral … in which by the permission of the dean and chapter the congregation of Saint John is wont to assemble … [we] think it our duty to remind you that when the Lady Chapel was lent to the congregation of Saint John it was with the implied condition that nothing should be allowed to take place there … which could compromise the chapter or be viewed by them with disapprobation … it is important therefore that care should be taken that the services in the Lady Chapel should not be conducted in a manner materially different from those in the cathedral.[33]

Two years later, the dean and chapter had to rap John Goss's knuckles yet again about his high church leanings. He had put an advertisement in the *Hereford Times* about a proposed service for the English Church Union, a society with Anglo-Catholic credentials. The dean and chapter dealt with this in a very diplomatic way, pointing out that permission could not be given 'as the service would clash with the parochial service', which it was clearly intended to do.[34] The dean and chapter must have wondered whether John Goss was deliberately being provocative. In November 1873, the Bishop of Hereford gave his 'express approval' to the Protestant Revival meetings that were taking place in the city. In the parish, where prayer and tea meetings were being well attended, the Revd Canon Jenkins had been working with John Goss, who 'could not have secured the assistance of a more zealous advocate of the cause'.[35] In reality John Goss, as a high church man, must have supported these meetings through gritted teeth. Perhaps this was yet another attempt by the dean and chapter to bring this theologically unruly vicar into line. However, John Goss would have found support for his own high church leanings in Sir Frederick Ouseley and John Jebb, who were both at the cathedral at that time and who were both 'committed to the ceremonial and liturgical revival of the Church of England'.[36]

John Goss had, of course, to deal with pastoral as well as spiritual issues, not all of which were pleasant. In May 1876, the *London Daily News* carried an article entitled *Immorality at Hereford*. It began, 'yesterday a meeting of clergy and laity was held in the Lady Chapel, under the presidency of the Rev. John Goss, to consider whether persons keeping disorderly houses in Gwynne Street should be indicted.' The article went on to say that the houses in question had been leased from the dean and chapter but were not, at the time the lease was signed, occupied by immoral people. However the lessee, Mr Mills, suggested 'that those who stalked through the streets in black broadcloth' were the frequenters of such houses. He offered to join the dean and chapter in suppressing the nuisance and said he had given his tenants notice to quit. When challenged to name the clergy who went to the houses, Mr Mills refused to do so. However, John Goss was at pains to make it clear that any such visits were entirely concerned with the spiritual welfare of the girls in the houses. He had himself 'removed a girl from temptation who lived near the houses, but it was difficult for clergy to perform their spiritual duties if so unfairly suspected. He should enter such places in future with fear and trembling, lest his mission be mistaken.' After charge and counter-charge about where the immorality rested, with the girls or the men in black broadcloth, the meeting merely resolved to ask Mr Mills to remove the tenants from the houses.[7]

Only three months after this report, another unpleasant incident, this time of an olfactory kind, occurred. Headed in the newspaper as 'scene at a pauper funeral', it told the story of the funeral of 59-year-old William Hartland, a pauper who, until his death, had been living in Gwynne Street. John Goss was officiating at the funeral when 'a very offensive smell arose from the coffin, and he noticed that the coffin was cracked from top to bottom.' Not only was the coffin inadequate, so were the bearers for, in a story worthy of Dickens, it seems that Hartland's landlord, who had promised to find bearers, had only 'furnished one woman, the gravedigger in his shirt sleeves and the driver of the Union hearse'. The story was reported to the members of the Board of Guardians, who were suitably astonished and indignant, calling in the coffin-maker and strongly censuring him.[38]

John Goss

There is a curious personal postscript to the life of John Goss. It would be easy to assume that he remained a rather argumentative bachelor, for he had appeared in the 1861 and 1871 censuses as living, unmarried, in the College of the vicars choral. Yet there was a wedding which, whilst not entirely secret, nevertheless holds some mystery. In April 1872, John Goss had officiated at the marriage in London of Alexander Jones, vicar of Moreton Jeffreys, Herefordshire, to Wilhelmina Cecilia, the eldest daughter of a George William Speth.[39] Three months later, in June 1872, the *Leamington Courier* carried the following marriage announcement:

> GOSS – SPETH. On the 19th instant, at St. Jude's, East Brixton … the Rev. John Goss, B.A., succentor of the cathedral and vicar of St. John, Hereford, eldest son of Sir John Goss, to Lucy Sarah, youngest daughter of George William Speth, Esq.[40]

Curiously, this announcement appeared in several other journals but not the Hereford newspapers. Yet Bishop James Atlay of Hereford officiated and so it could not have been a secret wedding. Was this, perhaps, a whirlwind romance – did this high church man, who might well have dedicated himself to a life of celibacy, fall in love at the earlier wedding with the younger daughter, who was 22 years his junior, and marry her after a brief courtship? And why was John Goss resident in Ilfracombe at the time of his marriage, rather than Hereford where he was employed?

By November 1873, John and Lucy Goss were living in the College of the vicars choral and it was there that their first daughter was born.[41] A year later, there was a long report in the Act books about the 'objection that the dean and chapter had long entertained to the residence of married vicars in college … especially in the case of those vicars having children.'[42] No wonder then that, three years later when a second daughter was born, it was in Ilfracombe.[43] The dislike of the dean and chapter for women and children cluttering up the College, with all the chatter and noise that they make, must have driven Lucy into more congenial surroundings for her confinement. However, both daughters were baptised by their father in St John's parish church.[44] In 1877, when Lucy was pregnant with their third child, John Goss died, aged only 51. His death was widely reported in the newspapers of the time and the *Hereford Times* printed an eulogy in which his passion for argument was set out at length. The paper commented that:

Alfred Capel

it is anything but a discredit to his memory to say that he relished beyond all things an opportunity of applying his acute mind and his argumentative tongue or pen to the solution of problems which weaker or more timid men would have left to the care of the lawyers … and Mr Goss undoubtedly had a very keen taste for buckling on his armour and descending into the field of battle.[45]

What an unhappy and difficult time it must have been for this young widow, who was a wife for only five years and who then had to bring up three young children on her own. For John Goss, short though his married life had been, belated conjugal happiness might well have brought much contentment to this rather argumentative vicar.

After the death of John Goss, Dean Herbert and the chapter must have wanted a less challenging man as vicar of the parish and, in November 1877, Reverend Alfred Capel was appointed. Capel was left with no illusions about how he should run his parish, for it was clear that the new vicar of St John's had to conform to the style of worship in the cathedral. He was instructed that:

1. The ritual of the cathedral should be followed in the celebration of Holy Communion and in the ornaments of the holy table. Candles only to be lit when required for light.

2. Long surplices and plain black stoles to be used by the vicar and his curate and by any officiating minister.

3. Holy Communion should only be offered once on Sundays and once on Holy Days each week.

4. No religious service should be held in the Lady Chapel in connection directly or indirectly with the English Church Union, the Society of the Holy Cross, or the Confraternity of the Blessed Sacrament (this last being another Anglo-Catholic body frowned upon by the dean and chapter).

5. Non-communicating attendants not to be encouraged.[46]

Despite these injunctions, there were a few peaceful years in the life of the parish, marked primarily by further beautifying of the Lady Chapel. In 1882, Alfred Capel presented the parish with 'the gift of a Litany desk … most exquisitely carved in oak'.[47] In 1885 altar rails, also very exquisitely carved in oak, were added.[48] However, like John Goss before him, Alfred Capel found himself having to cope with secular problems in the parish, one of which attracted widespread national interest. This was the affair of Robert Andrews, one of five lay clerks who had taken part in 'smoking concerts' in the Green Dragon Hotel. The dean and chapter felt that it was 'not desirable for lay members of the choir to take part in any entertainments where intoxicating liquors were sold' and he was, with the others, reprimanded.[49] However this was the least of his misdemeanours, for, as an assistant overseer for the parish, he was responsible for keeping the parish accounts. In the late summer of 1885 it emerged that he had been misappropriating parish funds for a considerable length of time and that he owed £574 13s 5d. Rather than face the consequences of his actions, on 18 December he left his home, wife and two young sons, ostensibly to sing at some concerts in Birmingham. He was never seen again. The *Hereford*

Times ran the story over several editions under the heading 'the mysterious disappearance from Hereford: serious defalcations'. The paper said that Mr Andrews' mysterious disappearance had been one of the principal topics of conversation in Hereford for many weeks, but it had now become clear that 'the missing man is a defaulter and that he has misappropriated a large sum of money. Mr Andrews seems to have commenced his career of dishonesty about twelve or thirteen months ago and it would appear that he has appropriated to his personal use sums of money which he had collected from the ratepayers in his capacity as assistant overseer.'[50]

By 6 February 1886, the local newspapers reported that a warrant had been taken out for Mr Andrews' arrest for which the vestry offered a substantial reward, as recorded in their minutes for 19 February.[51] It was, however, the belief of both the police and the general public that he had left the country and reports in October of the same year showed that he still had not been found.[52] A search in the newspapers for the following five years has revealed nothing. Robert Andrews seemed to have well and truly disappeared.

Later that same year, Alfred Capel was involved in another of the skirmishes that regularly occurred between the parish and chapter. This was in relation to the dorsal[53] that had been placed behind the altar in the Lady Chapel and which had been presented by:

> Mrs Bull, in memory of the late Doctor Bull, who for many years was a regular worshipper in this most beautiful edifice. As a work of art there is perhaps no piece of embroidery in the diocese to equal, and certainly not to surpass, Mrs Bull's gift. The dorsal is worked on white damask, the centre an Agnus Dei on a gold background with emblems of the four evangelists, on one side are figures of the Blessed virgin and child, and on the other is a representation of St John the Baptist.[54]

Henry Graves Bull (1818-85) was an eminent and well-loved Herefordian. He was an excellent doctor, and did much to improve health and sanitation in the county; he contributed regularly to the Woolhope Club *Transactions*, whilst his *Herefordshire Pomona*, an attempt a full catalogue of the varieties of apples and pears grown in the county, brought him national fame. It seems extraordinary that the dean and chapter would object to what seems to have been a very beautiful gift from his widow. Yet object they did, for they felt that they needed to inform the vicar of the parish:

> that everything placed there [in the Lady Chapel] by way of ornament, whether permanently fixed or not, should first be submitted to and sanctioned by them. For the future therefore they must insist that no further ornaments be introduced which have not been submitted to and approved by them, failing which they will be obliged to order the immediate removal of anything placed hereafter, however good in itself it may be.[55]

The dean and chapter might disapprove of ornaments, but that was not how the parishioners felt and they sided with their vicar, often decorating the Lady Chapel on high days and holidays. In December 1900, for example, the Lady Chapel 'looked very bright and lovely with its floral texts and foliage in celebration of Christmas ... although the morning was so dark and wretched there were 35 communicants at 7 a.m.'[56] Then, as now, the women of the parish were responsible for all this finery, the most local of them being the widow and four daughters of Henry Graves Bull. Imagine them, in the gloom of a winter afternoon, stepping out of their

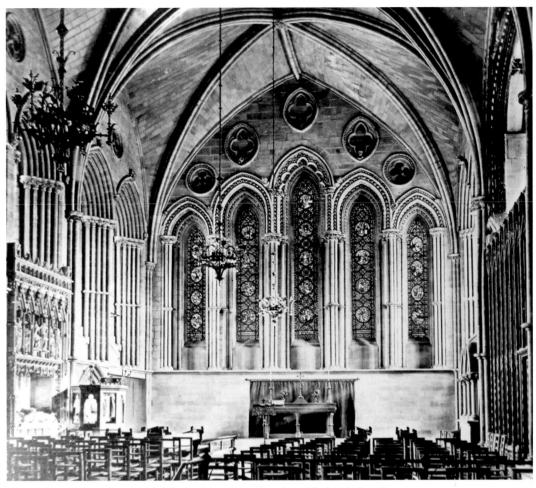

The Lady Chapel with a dorsal behind the altar

home in Harley House on the far side of the Close, and walking along the neatly swept walks, their long dresses rustling, to meet their companion flower arrangers who were, perhaps, after their labours, all invited back to take tea before returning to their own homes.

From Victoria to dissolution

Despite the sometimes irritated exchanges between the parish and the dean and chapter which appear in the written records, in reality, much of the latter part of the 19th century seems to have been a peaceful one for the parish. In October 1899, Joseph Carless, town clerk from 1868 until 1911 and a churchwarden in the parish, wrote that 'his association with the parish, as one of the churchwardens, for the long period of 21 years, was a happy one. It was an era of parochial peace which I trust may long be continued.'[57] Yet despite the love that many parishioners had for their church, several centuries of parish life were coming to an end. The population of the parish had been dropping slightly throughout the latter part of the 19th century, and, in 1918, the *Hereford Times* reported on the enthusiasm of the dean, James Wentworth Leigh, for reducing the parish boundaries. He said that:

the use of the Lady Chapel was granted by the dean and chapter to the vicar and parishioners. It was not the church of St John. It was the Lady Chapel of the church of St Mary. He favoured the new scheme, which had been well thought out. St John's was a very scattered parish, and it was proposed to add the little bits to other parishes.

The parishioners did not agree and Dean Leigh's comments must have led them to feel that 'their' parish altar was there under sufferance from the dean and chapter. Mr Bustin, a well-known local photographer of the time, who lived in Palace Yard, seemed to speak for his fellow parishioners when he said that 'things had gone on well for many years and he did not see why there should be any alterations. In any case, the parishioners should be consulted (hear, hear). He would be sorry to see any severance and hoped the parish of St John would long continue to exist (hear, hear).'[58] It was clear that the proposed change was greeted with both anger and sadness from parishioners.

Yet, a year later, the dean, James Wentworth Leigh made the same argument for boundary revision on the grounds that 'the parish of St John was widely scattered, without a parsonage house, or separate parish church, simply a prescriptive right to hold services in some part of the cathedral of Hereford.' The order was made to put the suggested scheme into effect. Most of the parish was divided between its neighbours, leaving little more than the area around the Close as the parish of St John. With this change, the parish, as such, virtually ceased to exist. It no longer had its own services, as they were merged with those of the cathedral.[59] Parish vicars were no longer appointed, with the role being merged with that of the dean of the cathedral, who thus became the vicar of the much reduced parish. The Lady Chapel was used not by parishioners but by the 'cathedral school for hymns and prayers every weekday and Matins on Sundays'.[60]

From this point on, the parish is rarely mentioned in the Act books, other than minuting a change of vicar when a new dean was appointed. In 1924, it was agreed that the services of the parish clerk be dispensed with 'in view of the fact that, since the parish had been reduced to its present dimensions and there no longer being any parish services held in the cathedral, there seemed to be few, if any, duties for a clerk to perform.' He did, however, continue to receive 'two pounds per annum for the sole duty for so long as he was able to perform it, of opening and closing the door before and after the Sunday morning service of the Cathedral school when that was held'.[61] The trappings of a parish remained – there was still a parochial church council and churchwardens. A discussion was held in 1925 and again in 1926 and 1928 about what to do with the worn-out items of parish furniture. The matter was left in abeyance and it then disappeared from view in the parochial minute book without any decision being made.[62] There was a last gasp of parish life as wedding certificates (with those few exceptions where the wedding took place in the cathedral itself) continued, until 2012, to give the 'parish church of St John the Baptist' as the place of marriage.[63] This would have been the Lady Chapel, as this was the final place of the parish altar in the cathedral; indeed most, although not all, marriages in the cathedral still take place there. Finally, after a century in which St John's was a parish in little more than name, on 17 May 2012, under the Pastoral Measures Act of 1983, which could be used to dissolve existing parishes, it was agreed that the 'benefice and parish of St John shall be dissolved'.[64] With this act, centuries of parish life and worship disappeared, without, it would seem, any obvious signs of regret or sadness.

4 LIFE IN THE PARISH TO ITS DISSOLUTION

> One of the frustrations of writing history is that dissension and controversy are recorded while the satisfactory daily life goes unnoticed.[1]

It is not until the accession of Queen Victoria, when the census returns, as well as parish registers, become available, that a fuller picture of the heyday of parish life emerges. At the time of the 1841 census, just over 1,000 people lived in the area of the parish adjoining the cathedral and, in terms of social origins, little had changed since the late medieval period. A third of the parish residents had been born in the city, a third in the county and a third in the country or, occasionally, abroad. Amongst the smattering of foreign workers were two Tuscans, both with exotic sounding names: Domenico Pisani was a civil and mechanical engineer apprentice, whilst Panacali Pellegrino was a plaster figure maker. The Green Dragon employed an Austrian waiter, Louis Lederer, a German waitress, Fanny Merly and a Swiss coachman, Marc Berthold. Louise Bally, another Swiss, was a lady's maid in the Bishop's Palace. It is easy to imagine that they all knew each other and that, when they had some free time, they would have been seen strolling in the Close in the summer sunshine. Robert Goetz, a German school master at the cathedral school, might have felt himself to be socially above these young people and perhaps was not part of their social circle. He was clearly a popular teacher for 'Herefordians old and young never had a more devoted friend and the school never a more zealous servant; when we think of Herr Goetz, it is as the friend to whom Old Herefordians turned on re-visiting the school.'[2] The old boys were so devoted to him that they later commissioned a portrait of him from Brian Hatton, the Hereford artist – a painting which now seems to have disappeared.[3]

Births, Marriages and Burials

At the top of the social scale, Catherine Mary Jane, the daughter of Sir Hungerford Hoskyns, Bt, the 7th baronet, and his wife Sarah, was, in 1815, baptised at the parish altar from a King Street address.[4] Quite why Sir Hungerford was having a child baptised from this address is unclear, for the Hoskyns family were at that time the owners of Harewood Park but presumably the house in King Street was their town base, enabling them to have the baptism at the parish altar and thus in the cathedral. Hungerford Hoskyns himself was a character:

> a sturdy man of the olden type, who rose at 6 a.m. to dig a portion of ground before breakfast, who daily drank the cider of his own orchards from a large silver tankard, and whose powerful voice could be heard at an unusual distance … he wooed and married his wife, a

gifted musician and a lady who endeared herself to rich and poor by her warm sympathy with all around her.[5]

At the other end of the social scale, the illegitimate children, as ever, came from the poorest streets and were born to the poorest women. During the Victorian period, Gwynne Street was home to 14 of the 18 baptisms of 'base' born children, although only one mother, Elizabeth Powell, a charwoman, had the courage to put 'unmarried' as her legal status on her census form. In 1871, Elizabeth was living in Gwynne Street with her four children: 10-year-old twins, born in the workhouse, a 3-year-old, born in Ross and a baby of seven months, born in the parish.[6] Nothing else is known about this family, as any records, such as those of the workhouse, no longer exist, leaving all sorts of unanswered questions. How had Elizabeth come to be in the workhouse and how did she get out; what had happened to the father or fathers of her children; how had she ended up in the parish? Whatever her situation, it is easy to imagine that, poorly dressed, with chapped, workaday hands, she crossed the Close each day to work for people in the grand houses in Castle Street, scrubbing and polishing for very little money in order to keep her children.

As well as baptisms, the parish church was often the setting for weddings; there were nearly 300 marriages in the years between 1839 and 1901. In a society in which a career path and independence for a women were not easy, marriage was generally seen as the proper purpose of a woman's life. Yet an unequal demography, with more woman of marriageable age than men, together with an exodus of men who went to work in the Empire, meant that there were spinsters aplenty in the country. Indeed, Mrs Gaskell based her 1851 novel *Cranford*, with its many spinsters, on observation rather than imagination. The parish reflected this unequal demography, for, in a ratio that changed little throughout the period, about a quarter of its female residents over 30 were unmarried. Although fewer men remained bachelors, they too tended to remain single until their 30s or later – Joseph Jones, a Quaker bookseller in Broad Street, for example, did not marry until well into his 40s, after which he and his wife produced five children.

Some wedding certificates give a glimpse into one particular aspect of Victorian society: that of the lack of education of many of the poorer members of the parish. In the parish marriage registers for 1837-93, a total of 22 women and 15 men signed the register with their mark, an X, rather than writing their name. In these cases, the women either did not work or were servants, whilst the men were mainly labourers. In ten cases, both bride and groom signed their name with a mark. These weddings were probably humble affairs, with the bride and bridegroom, both in their one 'best' outfit, walking across the Close and into the parish 'church' to be married before their families and friends; then going to a local hostelry for the merriment of a marriage feast. These parish weddings rarely attracted newspaper coverage, but one that did was in 1874, when it was attended by a grand crowd, with the Lady Chapel being:

> thronged by a large number of persons, chiefly young ladies … for the unusual occurrence of two weddings taking place in the same family, the brides being the daughters of Mr and Mrs Meats of Hunderton Hall, near this city; the bridegrooms were Mr W. Dutton, of Aylestone House, and Walter, eldest son of Mr Robinson, Baker Street, Portman Square, London.

Hunderton was one of the outlying areas of the parish, hence this Lady Chapel wedding. The account of the nuptials continued with a description of the arches erected at the home of the brides 'by workmen in token of their respect for the head of the family, as well as to show their esteem for the young brides'. A wedding breakfast was held for about 40 people, with enthusiastic 'healths' being drunk and speeches being given. The bridal couples left in the afternoon for their wedding tour, 'followed by the hearty good wishes of all, not forgetting the customary shower of old shoes'.[7]

However, never believe what you read in the newspapers, as the parish marriage register only listed two weddings for 19 March 1874 and the brides were not sisters. One certificate reads 'William Dutton: full age: bachelor, architect, [father] William Dutton, gentleman. Alice Wells Meats: full age: spinster, Hunderton, [father] John Meats farmer.' So far, so accurate, but the next entry reads 'Walter Byatt Robinson: full age, bachelor, warehouseman, Baker Street, Marylebone, London, [father] Richard Robinson, mercer. Ellen Payne: full age: spinster, Hunderton, [father] William Payne, hotel keeper.'[8] Rather than being sisters, might the two girls have been cousins or even best friends? Why did the paper get it so wrong? The information is, sadly, lacking. Certainly there is only one Meats marriage recorded on the ancestry website.

Whilst baptisms and weddings would have been happy affairs, the 500 or so burials in the parish would have been sad occasions. After the closure of the Close churchyard at the end of the 18th century, burials took place at Blackmarston, where, over the years, several incidents occurred, some grisly and some uplifting.[9] In 1832, the *Hereford Times* carried a report about body snatchers when 'a man was discovered between one and two o'clock on Thursday morning, in St John's burial ground at Blackmarston. The man was fired at before he had collected his forces, who were in attendance in the background. He made a hasty retreat and evaded pursuit.'[10]

A more uplifting event was the funeral, on 23 November 1860, of 67-year-old William Morris, an 'old sailor' and a resident at Coningsby Hospital. His remains were 'conveyed in a hearse for interment at St John's Burial Ground … and his corpse preceded to the grave by his brethren dressed in their scarlet attire, which caused the funeral to assume a novel appearance and to attract considerable attention.'[11] An even livelier funeral was that of another Coningsby resident, 91-year-old John Thomas, who was buried on 29 September 1866. He had seen:

A Coningsby resident pictured c.1910

a good deal of service at Copenhagen[12] and elsewhere, and had … expressed a strong desire to be buried in an oak coffin … he had deposited a £5 note in the hands of a well-known coffin-maker, who prepared the final tenement for him in the best style … his remains were followed to St John's burial ground by the Corporal and servitors of Coningsby Hospital, in their red cloaks, and also by the staff of the Herefordshire militia and several pensioners, accompanied by the drum and fife band.[13]

Even in an age of high infant mortality, the death of a hundred or so children before reaching their teenage years must have been a source of deep distress to parents. One of the saddest families in terms of young deaths was that of Richard Phillips, the Cathedral Close keeper for over 40 years. Five of the seven children born to his wife Elizabeth died at a very early age – Caroline, aged two, in 1872; Richard, aged five months in 1876; Eveline, aged three months in 1879; William, aged four months, in 1881; and Ethel, aged seven months, in May 1886.[14] It would have been a sad little family that regularly trooped across the Close for the children's funeral services. However,14 years after their last child was buried, there was much to celebrate in the Phillips family, as their two remaining daughters married within three months of each other, one to a prison officer and one to a police officer. Given that Richard Phillips was a constable, there was something of the 'keeping it in the family air' about these marriages.

One of the oddest addresses for the death of a baby was that for Hubert Cross who died in 1878 at 13 months and whose address was the Green Dragon Booking Office – shades of 'a handbag' in *The Importance of being Earnest*.[15] Well over 70 inmates of the workhouse also had parish funerals. These were probably, in some ways, the saddest funerals of all, with few people attending to mourn the deceased. Those who did have family to mourn them were refused the chance to show their grief with flowers or other symbols of mourning, since, at a meeting of the Hereford Union on 4 February 1860, it was resolved that 'the relieving officer should attend pauper burials and take care that the coffins are not decorated or ornamented by the friends of the deceased.'[16]

As the parish was so close to the river, death by drowning within its boundaries was not uncommon and, in cold winters, the local newspaper regularly reported the antics of the fool-hardy who had met their deaths by falling through the ice. In 1841, a Gwynne Street boy met such a death. It was a harsh January: 'frost had set in again, with increased severity … the ground was covered with snow … Thursday night was the coldest experienced for many years'.[17] The Wye was frozen and 16-year-old John Pugh was enjoying the thrill of skating on the river with his friend when the ice broke. He fell into the freezing, fast-flowing water and:

> in the surprise and agony of the moment uttered a few hurried cries for help, but quickly passed with the stream under the ice … his generous and kind companion, Jennings, in an instant scrambled to the assistance of the unfortunate creature, but nothing but his cap was seen to rise.[18]

John Pugh's father Thomas was a mason and a widower living, at the time of the 1841 census, with his four children. The burial of 45-year-old Ann Pugh, his wife, was recorded a year earlier.[19] Although it is not known where he worked, it is entirely possible that, living so close to the cathedral, he was employed on the renovations that had just been started. It is easy to imagine one of the younger children racing across the Close to give him the sad news and Thomas downing tools and hurrying home, only to find his drowned son's body laid out on a table. The inquest on this 'late melancholy accident on the ice' returned a verdict of accidental death, and it must have been a sad funeral in the parish church on a bitterly cold January day a few days later. It would have been doubly poignant as the children had lost their mother and Thomas a wife only a year earlier.[20]

Suicide and attempted suicide were also part of the life of the river. In July of the same year, a young lover made a botched suicide attempt, which led to his being named 'silly Billy' in the *Hereford Times*. William Brookes, a servant living in Gwynne Street, was in love with a young neighbour, Elizabeth Preece. In a Romeo-like action, he was waiting for his beloved in her father's garden at ten o'clock on a summer evening, but, instead of his lover, some 'unloving person' called a policeman appeared. This 'unsympathising animal' marched William out of the garden and across the nearby Wye Bridge.[21] As he did so, Billy, after quoting a few lines of doggerel that ended with 'but of all the pains, the greatest pain; it is to love – but love in vain', vaulted over the parapet of the bridge and would have plunged into the river, had not the quick-witted policeman caught him and held him fast. When he appeared before the bench for the crime of attempted suicide, the conversation went as follows:

> Magistrate: Did you intend to destroy yourself, or only cool your love?
> Silly Billy: Drown myself, *I suppose*; it was done on the spur of the moment.
> Magistrate: If we let you go now, will you promise to be a good boy, and never do so again?
> Silly Billy: I shouldn't, I *dare say*.
> Magistrate: Well, you are discharged, but recollect, if you make an attempt again, you will
>   probably have to be carried to the churchyard, instead of the police court.[22]

However, it was not the churchyard for William but a wedding for, in December of the same year, he married his sweetheart in the parish church. Attempted suicide, it seems, did the trick for young love.

What did people do?

As in earlier centuries, most of the parishioners in employment were men (and a handful of women) doing unskilled or semi-skilled jobs, with 'labourer' being the most common occupation. Employment in some occupations, such as those dealing with the basic practicalities of food, drink and clothing, remained steady throughout the period; others saw a decline, owing to more mechanisation and the fact that other parts of the city, such as High Town, had become the shopping hub. Thus, in the parish, the number of bakers declined from eight in 1841 to one by 1901; and butchers, who numbered as many as six in 1861, disappeared altogether by 1891.

Another dying trade was that of wool stapler. In 1841, William Cooke was one such; by 1851, he appeared as 'a wool stapler and butcher, late of King Street, now in the gaol as an insolvent debtor'.[23] By the end of the century, the wheelwrights, umbrella and trunk makers, tallow chandlers and soap boilers, leather dyers, hop assistants and dyers had also disappeared from the parish.

*One of James Wathen's sketches of the
River Wye at Hereford c.1800*

As for women, milliners and dress makers were found throughout the period, but by 1851 the four bonnet makers working in 1841, like the bargemen, had disappeared. The trades undertaken by women were sometimes surprising: there were labourers and butchers, a barge owner, a fishmonger, a currier, a taxidermist and a female mason who worked in marble. The last was Ann Jennings, who was unmarried but who could afford to employ two servants, 70-year-old Mary Grainger and 16-year-old Mary Hill. When he died in 1859 her father, Benjamin, had left her 'all my messuage and tenement in King Street … with the yard, workshop and other buildings … which I hold by lease from the custos and vicars of the College of Vicars.' He also left her all his household goods, furniture, plate, glass etc., as well as his 'wines spirituous liqueurs and stores and provisions for housekeeping'.[24]

Church Street c.1900

Broad Street c.1890 (courtesy of Marion Beddoe)

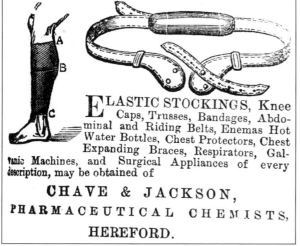

ELASTIC STOCKINGS, Knee Caps, Trusses, Bandages, Abdominal and Riding Belts, Enemas Hot Water Bottles, Chest Protectors, Chest Expanding Braces, Respirators, Galvanic Machines, and Surgical Appliances of every description, may be obtained of

CHAVE & JACKSON,
PHARMACEUTICAL CHEMISTS,
HEREFORD.

An advert in The Hereford Times *for 1871*
for Chave and Jackson

By the end of the Victorian era, new jobs and trades had appeared: there were railway labourers; an engine driver and engine cleaner; a post office superintendent, post master and postman; a student of mechanical engineering; a civil engineer; a cycle manufacturer; and a clerk in shorthand and typewriting.

Trades in Church Street, in particular, reflected the changing times: in 1871 there was a plate layer and a railway clerk; in 1881 the young Elizabeth Sexty worked in the telegraph department of the Civil Service; by 1901 the street was home to a racing stable boy and a gas fitter as well as an actor, Leonard Thackeray; whilst a cider agent reflected Hereford's fame as a cider making city. It was also home, throughout the period, to a number of people with cathedral connections, ranging from masons who were employed on the cathedral restoration; to Alban Moore, the cathedral sexton; to William Jennings, a verger; and to the cathedral organists, who lived at number 20 Church Street.

Broad Street was the busiest thoroughfare in the parish, home to about 200 or so people, ranging from tradespeople who ran businesses to the genteel man or woman, often living on independent means and employing some of those servants who made up about one fifth of the residents of the parish, a proportion of servants to 'others' that changed little over the 60 years between the 1841 and the 1901 census. Some businesses arrived that can still be seen today: William Chave, the chemist, had arrived by 1865 and William Oswin, the jeweller, by 1891.

Although now in King Street, Walter Pritchard's outfitters shop was in Broad Street in 1871. The following quotation from *Hereford Illustrated*, gives a real flavour of life for the well-to-do Herefordian at that time. It also illustrates a world that was changing fast, as the mass-production of goods ousted hand-made goods:

Messrs. W. Pritchard and Sons have ... a very large connection among the clergy, gentry and professional classes. Their shop ... contains an immense stock of cloths, suiting, tweeds

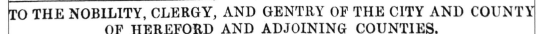
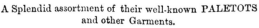
An advert in The Hereford Times *for 1881*
for Pritchard and MᶜMullen

and silk ... clerical, hard and soft felt hats, livery, ladies' silk and felt hats ... special outfits for tennis, cricket, boating, etc. are also provided ... dress suits, morning suits, riding breeches, hunting suits, etc. are all turned out in the perfection of good workmanship.[25]

The world of the tailors, however, was a far remove from those of the patrons of the clothes. An account by a descendant of the Pritchard family states that 'in those days 30 tailors worked cross-legged, chewing tobacco ... they had a secret method of removing the baccy stains from white buckskin breeches ... many were down and out types who were very fond of drink, and used to sleep on the premises.'[26]

As late as the 1850s, cattle would stroll down Broad Street to be sold at its market, their smells mingling with those of the tanners and skinners who lived and worked there. Although the trade in selling cattle in Broad Street ended in 1856, with the opening of the market in Newmarket Street, in 1858 a splendid Corn Exchange was opened so that some market activity, albeit less smelly and noisy, still occurred in the parish.

By the end of the Victorian period, Broad Street was also home to several inns including, by 1861, a Railway Inn, a sign of the changing times. As for coaching inns, there were two at the

Cattle on sale in Broad Street

start of the Victorian era: the Green Dragon and the Mitre.[27] The Mitre managed to capitalise on changing transport trends and, when the stage coach era ended, it became a popular venue for cyclists. By 1891 it was being run by the Williams sisters and was receiving high praise for its welcome and standards. It was:

> a very old and well-known house, with a long-established reputation ... it provides a home from home, the bedrooms, sitting, coffee, dining and commercial rooms are really models of quiet comfort ... the Misses Williams like nothing better than to offer a hearty welcome to the constant bands of touring cyclists, who make it their temporary abiding place.[28]

An inn that became a boarding house in the middle of the 19th century, before being demolished in 1935, was the Globe. In 1847, it was being run by Thomas Boulton who offered good stabling, well-aired beds and wines and spirits of the best quality. The Globe was often the scene of lively parties such as that given in 1860 for the retirement of William Bradford, the foreman of the cathedral works. A 'pleasant party' gathered to enjoy a 'dinner, which was beautifully and plenteously served up by Mr Boulton'. After dinner, the workmen, as a token of their esteem, begged Mr Bradford:

A Herefordshire cycling party, such as might have stayed at The Mitre

to accept this gold pencil-case and books, which are inscribed to yourself. May you long enjoy them and when you are no more may they descend as an heirloom to posterity, who we hope will cherish your memory as we shall when you are gone.

Mr Bradford responded with a speech of heartfelt thanks, and the evening was rounded off 'when conviviality set in with real earnest, and a most agreeable evening was spent'. Both the servants and Mr Boulton were kept very busy supplying their good beer, before the workmen took their various ways home in a very happy frame of mind.[29] It is likely that the three servants listed in the 1861 census were there by the time of this convivial party. Had they been, 13-year-old potboy George Evans would probably have been kept busy serving beer to thirsty customers, including the men working on the cathedral restoration. Mary Garstone, 19 years old, a general servant, was probably set to scrubbing and cleaning, as well as serving customers. Henry Morris was described in the census as a labourer and brewer and he was responsible for the good ale provided for the customers of the inn.

Pleasure, Punishment and Public Order
The Victorian parishioners would have had plenty of opportunities for relaxation. The parish had numerous public houses; the May fair filled the streets around the cathedral once a year; and, in 1874, the free library was opened. The Victorian passion for self and societal improvement meant that, in 1898, the *Hereford Times* was able to boast that, 'within the last half-century, a number of distinct advances had been made in the city, for it had an Infirmary and an Eye and Ear Hospital, a Working Boys Home and many other institutions doing good work for society and humanity.'[30]

Education of children was also of increasing importance in the parish.[31] There were, throughout the century, several small, privately run schools, such as Mrs Wright's in Castle Street, which offered, for the instruction of young ladies, 'reading, English grammar, elocution, writing, arithmetic, history, geography, plain and ornamental needlework, the French and Italian languages, music, drawing, &c.'[32] For young men, Mr Thomas Carpenter, of the Commercial School in Castle Street, offered his education in the following glowing terms. He asked the question: 'how can the agriculturalist and the tradesman know ... what best way they may educate their children?' His answer was that 'Greek and Latin will not be any great use either in the market or behind the counter, but a good commercial education is of the highest importance.'[33] These were only a few of the many small schools that were privately run but they would all have been fee paying and only those with a reasonable income could afford them.

However, in 1866, four years before the 1870 Education Act, which provided free educa-tion for all children between the ages of five and 13, John Goss asked the dean and chapter for permission to take over use of 'a billiard room and small house adjoining in Church Street to be let for a school'.[34] St John's school was opened in 1868 for 'the instruction of children and adults, or children only, of the labouring and manufacturing and other poorer classes.'[35] By 1871, it was able to 'accommodate 188 children, with a proposal to erect two additional rooms, which would accommodate 144 more and with a night-school being held in the largest room during the winter months.'[36] In 1881, Phoebe Rowlands, aged 26 and a 'schoolmistress at St John's', was living at 25 Church Street, a few doors away from 22-year-old Charles Hatton, a baker and confectioner. By 1891, Phoebe and Charles had married and had four children, ranging in age from one to six years. By this time, Charles was both a grocer's assistant and the parish clerk and Phoebe was still teaching, now being 'a certificated teacher of an elementary school'.[37]

Yet, despite all these advances, the parish still had its fair share of delinquent behaviour, and parishioners appear regularly in the local paper charged with offences that often resulted in harsh punishment, including transportation. The Close seemed to be a hot spot for delin-

The Close keeper's cottage, formerly the Mechanics Institute, on the left

51

quent behaviour and, by 1851, disorderly behaviour had become so serious there that the 'dean proposed that notice to quit be given to the tenant of the house called Mechanics Institute, with a view to placing someone in it connected with the cathedral to guard the Close.'[38]

In November 1851, William Clarke was appointed as the Close constable, charged with being available every evening from dusk to 11.30pm throughout the year, in order to prevent prostitutes and other improper people loitering in the Close. In addition he was to prevent noise and disturbance in the cathedral and the riot and disorder that went on nightly in the cathedral churchyard. He also had to assist in blowing the organ in the cathedral at morning and evening services.[39] When he was appointed, William Clarke was paid five shillings a week.[40] A year later his wages went up to twelve shillings a week – a massive jump.[41] It would seem that the difficulties of policing the Close were increasing, for, in the same year, there was a meeting between the dean and the city commissioners to discuss outbreaks of rowdy and immoral behaviour.

The gist of the dean's report to the commissioners was that a great many of the nuisances committed in the Close at night were due to a lack of adequate lighting. He cited as examples an incident when 'eight or ten women of the town and as many men came into the Close at night, and began to clap their hands and make dreadful noises'; and another when 'a man and a woman were seen to be behaving very indecently', adding that 'it should be remembered that at 10 or 11 o'clock at night few respectable people are about and the streets are left to a loose class who infest every town.' But, as so often with committees, there were more words than action and indeed there was clear resistance to change, with a member of the committee commenting that 'Hereford is Hereford and it ought to remain Hereford'. All that happened as a result of the dean's concerns was that a lamp in Quay Lane and one in Church Street were left on for a longer period.[42]

Poverty and Parish Relief

As in earlier centuries, the care of the poor continued to be the concern of both city and parish, with several establishments being set up to aid the poor. Victorian moral attitudes can be seen in the terms used for those who needed assistance: there were a Society for Aiding the Industrious (the 'deserving' poor who wanted to improve their situation);[43] a Home for Penitents; a Society for the Rescue and Protection of Young Women and Children (the 'fallen' poor in which women and children were reclaimed for respectable society); the Working Boys Homes (in which young boys were trained for employment); and last, but not least, the dreaded workhouse.

Charity often came with moral strictures attached, as in 1798 when Henry Hughes was apprenticed for seven years in the sum of £10 to Thomas Wilkes, 'turner and chair maker'. He was not allowed to 'commit fornication nor contract matrimony … play at cards, dice tables or any unlawful games … he shall not haunt taverns or playhouses, nor absent himself from his master's services.' In return, Thomas Wilkes was to instruct him in his art and to provide 'meat, drink, washing, lodging and other necessaries during the said term'.[44] It seems a rather tough set of rules. Sometimes the inhabitants of the parish clubbed together to raise money for aid. In October 1809 the *Hereford Journal* reported that:

> the inhabitants of St John's Parish have subscribed a sum sufficient to distribute to every
> poor person in the Parish, grown up, One Hundred Coals, One Loaf of Bread, One

Shilling to buy Meat and Beer; and to the poor children One Loaf of Bread, and Sixpence each, to buy Meat and Beer.[45]

The way in which parishioners discharged their responsibilities for the welfare of the poor varied enormously from parish to parish, with St John's parish holding a 'balanced view; relief was granted depending on the level of distress proved by the enquiries and, of course, the character of the applicant.'[46] It was at the vestry meetings that poverty in the parish was addressed. Before the passing of the Poor Law Amendment Act in 1834, the minutes are full of detail about charitable bequests made by the parish: sometimes it was money, sometimes bedding, coal or clothing.[47] The reason for the grant was never given, but typical grants were those to Sarah White, who was allowed two shifts, two pairs of stockings, two petticoats and a pair of shoes; William Wharton was allowed a smock frock[48] and Elizabeth Porter given a guinea so that she could be instructed in washing and ironing.[49] In 1828, Mrs Bagnall was allowed one pint of ale per day.[50] In 1832, Anne Llewellyn was given a very generous allowance of two calico shifts, a flannel petticoat, a linsey (a coarse linen or inferior wool) petticoat, two pairs of stockings, a pair of shoes, a pair of stays, a linsey gown, two neck handkerchiefs, a common bonnet and two common caps.[51]

The 1834 Act abolished outdoor relief and, although some help in cash or kind continued to be given, there was a sharp decrease in charity being doled out by the parish. Instead, parishes joined together to open workhouses for the reception and relief of vagrants and the 'undeserving' poor. The management of poor relief was given over to Boards of Guardians, who administered the affairs of a group of parishes and from this date a standard poor rate was set. The rates were for various parish needs: a proportion for the watch rate, and others for care of the church and churchyard, as well as the relief of the poor. As well as churchwardens, sidesmen and overseers, a surveyor and surgeon were appointed to the parish. Compassion was often shown by the overseers who sometimes excused parish residents payment of their poor rate assessment on the grounds of their poverty; sometimes they were not just poor, but 'poor and miserable', or 'destitute, old and poor', or 'poor and nearly blind'. In 1841, Mrs Watkins was excused as her husband had been transported. This was probably Henry Watkins who, on 22 May 1841, was sentenced to seven years' transportation for stealing a pair of women's boots.[52] The overseers also had to police the behaviour of the poor for, in 1862, they provided a list of the poor who had been set to work, the number of apprentices indentured, rogues and vagabonds punished and the number who were selling ale without licence.[53]

Prior to the opening of the Union Workhouse, in which conditions were to be made harsher than those for the lowest paid of workers, there were three workhouses in the city; two of these were retained until a new workhouse could be built. The one in All Saints was used for able-bodied males and the one in St John's 'for all other classes of pauper'.[54] This workhouse, the site of which it has not been possible to track down, had room for 'sixteen double beds plus the matron's quarters'.[55] There are occasional references in the vestry minutes to the upkeep of the workhouse, one of the most interesting being when the front parlour was 'tinselled by Tippins'.[56] It seems hard to imagine a workhouse having something as splendid as a front parlour being decorated with gold or silver leaf, but the guardians and other illustrious visitors would probably be shown into it when they visited to inspect the workhouse and its residents. In 1824, the matron, Mrs Jennings, was paid 4s 6d a week but not allowed to keep a dog.[57] The vestry had the power to arrange for people to be sent into, or removed from, the workhouse. In 1824, widow Price was 'allowed 1s per week till she is removed to the workhouse but that she be removed as soon as possible and that when she is removed 2s per week be added to her former allowance.' Yet, despite this, six months later her two boys were 'sent to the poor house till they can be provided for in the country or some other eligible situation'.[58] Imagine what they must have felt. Their father had died, and now they were being removed from their mother to a bleak and harsh regime in the workhouse, with no idea of what their future would hold. As so often, the outcome is not given.

The luckier ones who were removed from the workhouse were usually given money, bedding and clothes in order to help them settle back into the parish. For the unlucky ones, it was the other way round. In 1871, Julia and Richard Bryant were living in Gwynne Street with their parents and two brothers. The family must have fallen on hard times as, by 1881, Julia and Richard were both in the workhouse – Julia, aged 12, was a scholar and domestic worker; Richard, aged 15, was a clerk. The rest of the family had disappeared from view, or at least from the St John census.

Given the wealth of material for this period, it is easy, with a little imagination, to visualise the streets around the cathedral in the Victorian era. In the Close, people would have made their way into the cathedral for special events, such as the triennial Three Choirs Festival, solemn occasions, such as the funerals of clergy and their families, as well as the merriment of marriage. On a daily basis, the dean would stroll from the Deanery to the cathedral, servants would hurry to the shops, coachmen would sit, smart in their livery, behind prancing horses, school boys would rush about when school was out, whilst working men (and occasionally women) would be out in the early hours to go about their business in the city. Away from the bustle of the streets, in the dark office of a solicitor, a scratching pen or the hiss of a gas lamp might have been the loudest sound. This story of life in the parish has, so far, been a broad brush one. In the remaining chapters, stories of a handful of those people who lived in the parish, and whose lives can be traced from records, newspapers and the census, will be told. Sometimes sad, occasionally delinquent, often eccentric, their lives were always interesting.

5 THE SILVERSMITH, THE RECLUSE & THE BANK MANAGER

I am not a proper biographer ... my interest has always been in writing biographies of the
also-rans, people who ... since their deaths have sunk into profound obscurity.[1]

The three characters in this chapter have tenuous links to each other in that they all lived in
Broad Street in the early part of the Victorian period. The silversmith Solomon Lazarus (1793-
1845) is of interest, since in the Victorian era he was probably the only Jewish resident in the
parish. Chandos Hoskyns (1779-1862), the second son of Sir Hungerford Hoskyns, Bt, the
6th baronet, was born at the family home at Harewood End in Herefordshire, but lived a
reclusive life in Hereford for most of his adult life.[2] Frederick Hoskyns Matthews (1798-1883)
shared much in common with Chandos Hoskyns, including part of his name. Both came from
a gentry background, neither married, and both appeared to live frugal lives without servants.
They were also neighbours, but there the similarity ends, for, whilst Chandos Hoskyns seemed
gentle and courteous, Frederick Matthews, a failed banker, was an eccentric given to aggressive
outbursts.

Solomon Lazarus first appeared in the 1841 census, when he was living with his wife in
Broad Street. He had been 'born outside the county but not in foreign parts'.[3] He might well
have been born in Gloucester and gone back there to marry Sarah, the daughter of Moses
Levi, a silversmith, in 1812, for the wedding announcement stated that they were 'both of
Gloucester'.[4] In the 19th century, the Jewish community in Gloucester suffered from a steady
decline in numbers, with many moving to the expanding spa town of Cheltenham.[5] Solomon,
however, chose to settle in Hereford. He must have done so by 1811, when he was only 18. In
1825, in this advertisement in the *Hereford Journal*, he was thanking his clientèle for 14 years
of custom:

ELEGANT NEW AND SECOND-HAND
CHASED AND PLAIN SILVER PLATE.
Solomon Lazarus begs most respectfully to return
his sincere Thanks to his most numerous Friends for the
very liberal Encouragement he has received for the past Fourteen
Years, and at the same time to inform them that he has now by
him a LARGE STOCK of very elegant CHASED and other
PLATE, also a good Assortment of GOLD and SILVER
WATCHES, with DIAMOND RINGS and JEWELLERY
of every description, which he is determined to offer on such

Terms that no Person can undersell him, having recently purchased
the whole of his present Stock for Cash, in the best Market.
OLD GOLD AND SILVER TAKEN IN
EXCHANGE, or the most Money given for the same.[6]

A year later he informed the citizenry of Hereford that he had just returned from London where, 'owing to the depression of trade', he had purchased stock that he could sell from 10 to 15 per cent lower than the regular trade price. This stock included tea and coffee pots, waiters (trays or salvers), spoons and forks, liquor-stands, cruet-frames, sauce boats, etc. He also had jewellery, clocks and fancy goods, elegant hall lamps, fine cut glass wine decanters, rosewood writing desks, and watches 'by the best makers, some of them inlaid with pearls'.[7] Solomon Lazarus seems to have been a man with good business acumen, and his elegant wares must have been popular among the gentry and aspiring middle class inhabitants of the city. There is even one receipt with his signature when he did a part exchange, receiving from 'Captain Patteshall the sum of ten pounds ten shillings with two old watches in exchange for a gold watch valued £18'.

Solomon Lazarus was also, as were many of the Jewish community at that time, a pawn-broker and one, it seems, with a soft heart.[8] In 1831, he was asked to accept some gloves from Susan Cross. Although he knew the gloves were not hers to pawn, as they were owned by her master, he nevertheless advanced her half-a-crown 'out of charity, so that she could redeem a gown which was in pawn, and which she wanted to go to church on Sunday'. Susan had promised to redeem the gloves the following day but she had not done so, despite the fact that Lazarus threatened to tell her employer. As a result, Solomon Lazarus was convicted of illegal pawnbroking and, although the case was later quashed, there was a sting in the tail, as the court refused Solomon Lazarus his costs.[9]

In 1836, Solomon Lazarus was in court again, in another case of stolen property which had been pawned with him. John Perks, aged 20, and William Baldwin, aged 17, were charged with stealing 'a fustian jacket, a pair of cord breeches and some other articles of wearing apparel' from Thomas Birch, a labourer. Solomon Lazarus duly advanced them 12 shillings for these items of clothing, which seems a very handsome sum indeed. However Thomas Birch, in a hunt for his missing goods, went to Hereford and found them in Solomon Lazarus' house; the police were called and the men arrested. Despite the fact 'that several witnesses gave the men a good character' they were found guilty and sentenced to transportation for seven years. At the news

Receipt signed by Solomon Lazarus in 1828

of this sentence, 'two or three females left the court, and their shrieks were distinctly heard for several minutes afterwards'.[10]

By 1841, Solomon Lazarus had a curious side-line, acting as an agent for a firm of dentists. He arranged to have rooms available for 14 days at a time for A.S. Hart, a London dentist, who had available 'indestructible teeth, which far surpass any others ... for beauty and perfection of appearance and extreme durability, as they never decay, or change colour.'[11] It does seem an odd line of business for a silversmith, but silver was used in amalgam fillings at that time, and he might well have supplied some to Mr Hart. Or was it, perhaps, just that times were hard?

In March 1845, as he was to retire, he advertised that his business was for sale. Perhaps he was already ill, for he died, aged only 52, on 18 December of the same year. As an orthodox Jew, he was buried in the Jewish cemetery in Cheltenham, where a somewhat illegible headstone can still be seen. The parts that are legible read in translation from the Hebrew:

> Here lies buried ... may his soul be bound up in the bond of eternal life. Sacred to the memory of Solomon Lazarus of Hereford who departed this life on the ... 5605[12] [the Hebrew year 5605 started on the evening before September 14 1844 and ended on 1st October 1845].

Solomon Lazarus was not only a kind-hearted pawnbroker but also a generous contributor to many worthy causes in the city. His name appeared regularly in the local papers in relation to such gifts. The following examples in 1840 give some idea of his concerns. In January he gave 10s for the relief of the poor of the city,[13] in April it was 5s for the upkeep of the public walks on Castle Green,[14] in June he was at a dinner which raised money for 'clothing and apprenticing poor children, natives of Herefordshire', donating one guinea to the cause.[15] He also gave money for the purpose 'of erecting a new synagogue in Cheltenham'.[16] When he died, his obituary stated that he was 'for many years a highly respected inhabitant of this city. The poor, in him, will have to deplore the loss of a kind friend and benefactor, and his memory will long be cherished by his sorrowing friends.'[17]

What never appeared in his advertisements was the fact that Solomon Lazarus was also a clock maker. In *Clocks Magazine* in December 1990, under *Auctions*, it was reported that 'a low £495 secured a Regency mahogany striking bracket clock by Lazarus of Hereford, 1ft 7in high and with an 8in convex dial with strike/silent in the arch.'[18] Whether he made the entire clock or simply put the parts together is not clear, but it is with this clock that memories of Solomon Lazarus linger faintly into the 21st century.

Chandos Hoskyns shared a philanthropic spirit with Solomon Lazarus but there the similarity ends. He is, however, something of an enigma, having only the most succinct of entries in Burke's peerage: 'Chandos d. 5 December 1862'.[19] His father was, according to a miniature of him, 'a handsome man in scarlet coat, powder and pigtail of the period'; whilst his mother was a 'dainty lady' who wrote 'tender letters to her schoolboy sons as to the perils of their journey by coach to London'.[20] As a young man he moved to London and was, for many years, a Captain in the East Middlesex (Volunteer) Militia. He returned from London when still comparatively young and lived quietly and, it would seem, reclusively in Hereford for the rest of his life. In the

1841 census he was listed as living alone, describing himself as being of 'independent means'. For someone of his class to be without a servant or a housekeeper was odd, as he was living in an age when employing a servant was the norm for all but the poorest people. It was 'an age of servants. Households had servants the way modern people have appliances. Common labourers had servants. Sometimes even servants had servants.'[21]

By 1851, when he was 71 years old, Chandos Hoskyns described himself as a 'gentleman fund holder' but he was still living alone without any servants. By 1861 he described himself as a 'landed proprietor'. He also had his unmarried 40-year-old niece Caroline living with him. Still no servants, but perhaps she was acting as housekeeper for him. Like Solomon Lazarus, his name often appeared in the *Hereford Journal* and *Hereford Times* as someone who was involved in 'good works', such as being a member of the Committee of the Church Missionary Society;[22] the Hereford Protestant Association;[23] the Herefordshire Friendly Society;[24] The Industrial Aid Society[22] and others too numerous to list. He contributed to the Relief of Clergy in Ireland,[23] and to the fund for building a new church for the parish of Saint Nicholas.[27] He was also concerned with missions to the Jews, and attended the annual meeting of the London Society for promoting Christianity amongst the Jews in October 1855.[28] It would be interesting to know whether he ever tried to convert Solomon Lazarus or whether these two men, very different in both age and religious affiliation, but near neighbours, ever sat together over a glass of wine and debated religion and philosophy in a spirit of curiosity and tolerance.

Chandos Hoskyns was related to the Arkwright family of Hampton Court in Herefordshire through the marriage, in 1830, of his niece, Sarah, to John Arkwright. In the Arkwright archives, there is a good deal of material relating to the Hoskyns of Harewood End but, sadly, virtually nothing about Chandos. The two letters that do exist are those of a man of deep integrity and affection. Both letters refer to the fact that he would not transfer his railway shares in the Hereford, Ross and Gloucester railway to Arkwright, as they were worth so little. 'I would not want to throw the burden of my railroad shares upon your shoulders, knowing them to be good for nothing ... my love to all your house. Wishing you all a happy new year, believe me, yours very sincerely and affectionately, Chandos Hoskyns.'[29]

One curiosity, in the local newspaper in 1859, was to find Chandos Hoskyns giving a testimonial to Mr Anderson, a local surgeon-chiropodist, who removed 'corns, bunions, callosities, and defective toe nails in two minutes, by a method peculiar to himself without inflicting the slightest pain.' Amongst the many testimonials from Hereford worthies, Chandos Hoskyns wrote that Mr Anderson had 'removed corns and defective toe nails from my feet without pain and to my satisfaction'.[30] As he was 80 by this time, it is perhaps not surprising that he needed the attentions of a chiropodist. When Chandos Hoskyns died, he was buried in the family vault at Harewood End, with members of the family and 'several old servants' being present. His obituary in the local paper reinforced the sense of a reclusive, modest person who was:

a gentleman of large Christian sympathies and benevolence, dispensed with that unostentatiousness of manner which marked his character ... he lived in comparative retirement, but his life was one of such consistent piety, of such unostentatious charity, and of such scrupulous honour and integrity, that few were as well known amongst us, and as much esteemed and beloved as he was ... he was a member of the Church of England and his views were those of the Evangelical school ... greatly will he be missed by the poor, and by the conductors of numerous religious and charitable institutions both here and elsewhere.[31]

He sounds like a person one might wish to know. By contrast, Frederick Hoskyns Matthews was both aggressive and eccentric. His father, who served the city for many years as an alderman, mayor, and magistrate, was Dr John Matthews, a 'physician and poet'. He was also the Member of Parliament for Herefordshire from 1803-06 and Colonel of the first regiment of Hereford militia. Although he was at one time wealthy enough to build Belmont House, as 'a man of versatile disposition and generous tastes', he published poetry which often left him at a finan-

The City and County Bank in Broad Street c.1865

A banknote of The City and County Bank.
Note the images used are of the cathedral, the Shire Hall
and the base of the Blackfriars preaching cross

cial loss. Much of his work was badly received, some of it even being described as 'contempt-ible'.[32] It would seem that Frederick Hoskyns Matthews, his youngest son, followed in his father's footsteps, for he too was an indifferent author.

Frederick Hoskyns Matthews and his brother, John, were partners in the City and County Bank, 'one of the two old-fashioned banks of the city'. It issued its own bank notes and 'although most Hereford people had little confidence in it ... it did a fairly good business.' John Matthews died in 1849, leaving the 'principal part of his fortune to his brother and only partner'.[33]

However, Frederick Hoskyns Matthews was not a good businessman and, on 4 July 1863, the *Hereford Times* reported that:

> had a terrible thunder-cloud burst over Hereford on Saturday morning the explosion would not have excited the inhabitants of the city nearly so much as the ... report that the Herefordshire Banking Company did not intend to re-open their doors; and as the hour of ten approached that anxiety became intense ... copies of the following notices were placed in the windows: this bank is closed until arrangements CAN BE MADE WITH THE SHAREHOLDERS.

The reason for this abrupt closure was that the bank's London agents had refused to go on honouring their bank drafts. The report continued: 'Mr Matthews belongs to one of the most talented and respected families in the country; and as a proof of his honourable desire to preserve the commercial integrity of the bank he has ... disposed of £45,000 to fill the gap occasioned by losses from the failure of the large city traders.'[34] A week later, the *Hereford Times* reported that Frederick Hoskyns Matthews had been adjudged bankrupt. However, by August, the bankruptcy was annulled, as he had arranged for all the creditors to be paid.[35] Despite this, his banking career was over. Although it seemed a sad end to a career, Hoskyns Matthews had never been cut out for banking, being:

> utterly unfitted to control the affairs of a Bank, so that an old man named Hughes managed its business in a very primitive way ... Matthews himself was said to be one of the most curious personages in Hereford ... usually appearing in a somewhat ample cloak with his left elbow protruding under it ... the small street boys used to call him 'Teapot' when they saw him at a safe distance, but instead of simply ignoring their impudence, he would run after them ... his speed was quite wonderful ... and a boy was not only poked at with the point of the umbrella, but also belaboured with it over his back and shoulders.[36]

Three years later, Hoskyns Matthews suffered further ignominy when he was struck off the list of voters for the city.[37] Twelve years later, his name was again in the newspapers, when his book *Fragments and Fancies* was published. The *Pall Mall Gazette* was scathing:

> the writer has the aptitude for verse-making which is liable to deceive many ambitious young men; Mr Matthews, however, by his own confession, is no longer young, and therefore should have learned to estimate these clever trifles at their proper value. There is not one of them that bear the sign of poetical vitality ... [he] is a punster in verse, although some of his stanzas are marked by a not unpleasing banter.[38]

The last comment could be seen as 'damning with faint praise' but perhaps Frederick Hoskyns Matthews has, metaphorically, had the last laugh for, in 2011, the British Library, as part of its Historical Print Editions, re-printed his book.[39]

Being made bankrupt was one ignominy; being struck off the voting register another; perhaps the final one for this eccentric man was being summoned for assault. Hoskyns Matthews had moved to Bristol by 1880, and in June of that year, the *Bristol Mercury* reported under the heading 'Assault at Clifton College' that Frederick Hoskyns Matthews:

> an elderly gentleman, was summoned for assaulting and beating Francis George White, one of the pupils of the college ... a cricket match was being played when the defendant, who was watching the game, was told by one of the masters to leave the ground. He asked the complainant [White] to tell him the name of the master, but White, acting on instructions he had previously received, did not reply, whereupon Mr Matthews struck him over the head with a stick. The blow stunned the lad, and he fell into the arms of one of the masters ... the bench felt that that the old gentleman must not be permitted to behave in the way he had done.

Matthews was bound over in the sum of £10 to keep the peace for six months.[40] Three years later, the notice of his death was reported: 'January 8 at Clifton, Frederick Hoskyns Matthews, youngest son of the late John Matthews, Esq., of Belmont, near Hereford, aged 84.'[41]

There is sadness about all three of these men. Solomon Lazarus was still young when he died, apparently without issue; Chandos Hoskyns might well have been a lonely as well as a reclusive man; whilst the eccentric Hoskyns Mathews seems to have been an angry and unhappy man. Happiness, it seems, does not make headlines.

6 The Clairvoyant, the Manure Manufacturer & the Dancing Master

> Perhaps the time will come when one may be permitted to do research into the lives of ordinary people ... people who have no claim to fame whatsoever.[1]

The three very different characters in this chapter all seem to have in common charm and charisma, but also a tendency to deception. George Barnard Eagle deceived his gullible audiences by sleight of hand in his shows; Andrew Rowan made extravagant claims for his products; whilst Robert Vaughan was often in conflict with the law over aggressive dealings in his business.

George Barnard Eagle was only briefly resident in Hereford but he is included because he is probably the only clairvoyant to have been married at the parish altar. On 14 April 1844, he married a dressmaker, Hannah Edwards, both of them resident at the time in Church Street. On the marriage certificate George Eagle gave his occupation as that of comedian, but, in the newspaper announcement of the marriage, he had become 'Mr Barnardo [with an 'o'] Eagle, known as the celebrated 'Wizard of the South'. It turns out that this comedian was, in fact, a conjurer and a professor of clairvoyance.[2] Why the difference between these two announcements? No doubt he was afraid that, as a clairvoyant, he might well be refused a church marriage but, being eager to boast of his true credentials, they were included in the newspaper announcement of his nuptials.

George Eagle was born in London in 1807 and grew up to be a flamboyant conjurer and clairvoyant, who made a living by touring provincial theatres. He was clearly a skilled publicist as wherever he went he seemed able to persuade most of the people in his audiences of the veracity of his acts. By 1844 he was in Hereford, a widower, accompanied by his young son George and his daughter Georgiana, who was used as his partner in his shows.[3] Although there is no clue as to how and when he met his bride-to-be, it is perhaps not surprising that this peripatetic man, with two young children to look after, should be seeking another wife. Perhaps Hannah Edwards was captivated by his charisma during his shows, marrying him only weeks later. She was his junior by 14 years and only 10 years older than her step-daughter, Georgiana.[4]

When he performed in Hereford a few weeks before his marriage, George Eagle certainly did not stint on his publicity, as can be seen from this advertisement in the *Hereford Journal* announcing his attendance at the Assembly rooms in the City Arms hotel, commencing on Tuesday 26 March 1844.

The City Arms Hotel, now Barclays Bank

POSITIVELY FOR SIX NIGHTS ONLY
MR BARNARDO EAGLE
THE ROYAL WIZARD OF THE SOUTH

with his splendid **PALACE OF NECROMANCY** or scenes of fairyland, and Grand Entertainment of Scientific Magic, which totally obliterates all former efforts. The **CABALISTIC WONDER** he has created in London, Edinburgh, Glasgow, Liverpool, and Dublin has set these cities in a blaze of wonder and admiration … to which he has added a number of New Delusions, that will insure him the success which it is his pride at all times to deserve … in addition **MISS GEORGIANA EAGLE** the only **FEMALE ILLUSIONIST** in the world will introduce her new and novel performance, entitled **OCCULTOMACY OR INVISIBLE VISION.** The **WIZARDS** Splendid **BRASS BAND and CARRIAGE** will parade the Town previous to opening, and his **QUADRILLE BAND** will accompany the Entertainments.[5]

A week later, the *Journal* announced that the 'Wizard of the South' had been fascinating large numbers of spectators who had crowded the Assembly Rooms every evening of the week to witness his performance. After this show, George Eagle left Hereford with his new wife and continued his peripatetic lifestyle.

Seven years later, in December 1851, George Eagle was back in the area although not, it seems in Hereford. Although this time in Ludlow, the *Hereford Times* reported on 'that mystifying delusion of all delusions', the 'inexhaustible bottle, from which the Professor produces 100 glasses of all kinds of wines, brandy, rum, gin and whisky. This extraordinary feat was lately performed before Her Majesty at Balmoral, Scotland.'[6] A week later he was in Kington, 'exhibiting his very clever acts of deception and sleight of hand'.[7] He also decorated his stage with pictures of Georgiana, apparently receiving a splendid watch from Queen Victoria.

This would seem to indicate that Georgiana had some influence on Queen Victoria who was, as were many of her subjects, fascinated by the paranormal. However the reference to Georgiana receiving a splendid gold watch from Queen Victoria is an odd one. Although this watch did actually exist, eventually finding its way to the College of Psychic Studies, where it was exhibited for many years, there is nothing in Queen Victoria's diaries and correspondence to support this claim and at least one of Queen Victoria's biographers suggests it was fraudulent.[8] On the other hand, 'there have always been many clairvoyants who practise solely in private … such a person could have given meritorious clairvoyance to Queen Victoria without there being any special or royal writing to record the fact.'[9] It is impossible to know the truth of this story, but the claims were probably another part of the web of fantasy and magic that George and his daughter wove for their, it has to be said, gullible audiences.

Although the 'wizard' had many admirers, there were often those in his audiences who thought that 'George Eagle was the cleverest humbug they had ever seen'.[10] Yet, even though most people probably knew that the act was one of deception, George Eagle went on finding work until his death in Guernsey in May 1858.[11] He died on stage, having ruptured a large blood vessel in the region of his liver.[12] In what might be regarded as a slightly cynical note the *Ipswich Journal*, reporting the death, noted that 'the clairvoyance of Miss Eagle was not sufficient to foresee this event'.[13]

The next character in this chapter, Andrew Rowan, lived in Broad Street at the same time as the silversmith Solomon Lazarus and no doubt the two men would have known each other.[14] They might even have both attended George Eagle's show. Although Andrew Rowan was born in Belfast, he must have lived in Scarborough in the 1830s, as three of his children were born there. However by the time of the 1841 census, when he was 33 years of age, he was living in Broad Street with his wife Sarah and their five young children. He appeared to live in the same house as Thomas Inglis and, in the census, both men described themselves as hatters. He was clearly an entrepreneur, as can be seen from this advertisement in the *Hereford Times* in 1841, when, along with their hatting and hosiery trade, he and Inglis were appointed as the sole agents for a light waterproof coat for those intrepid travellers who went in search of picturesque landscape. Interestingly, the adver-

THE RECENT DISCOVERIES OF SCIENCE AND ART COMBINED
FOR THE BENEFIT OF THE
LOVERS OF THE PICTURESQUE,
Who must hail with delight every improvement which makes
COMMUNICATION EASY AND TRAVELLING AGREEABLE.
In an age like this, when Railways and Steamers connect the most
BEAUTIFUL AND ROMANTIC PARTS OF OUR ISLAND
with the busy haunts of " town imprisoned men," every inducement is offered to rusticate a few days among the
FERTILE VALLEYS OF OLD ENGLAND ;
or, by extending the trip, revel with delight among the MAJESTIC SCENERY of the
"LAND OF MOUNTAIN AND FLOOD;"
especially when this can be done with perfect security against wind and weather, without the inconvenience of a multiplicity of garments, the latter being superseded by the most elegant and useful
ZEPHYR WATERPROOF COAT,
ITS (ALMOST INCREDIBLE) WEIGHT BEING ONLY TWENTY OUNCES,
MADE BY
J. C. WARD AND CO.,
WHO HAVE APPOINTED
ROWAN AND INGLIS,
(NEARLY OPPOSITE THE GREEN DRAGON, BROAD STREET, HEREFORD,)
HATTERS, HOSIERS, &c.,
THEIR SOLE AGENTS.

An extract from The Hereford Times
for 12 June 1841

tisement refers to railways, but the Herefordians of 1841 had to wait another 12 years before they were able to get away from Hereford on a train.

Andrew Rowan was, it seems, keen to better himself for, by 1843, he was also studying for a medical qualification offered by the Erlangen University in Bavaria. However, this MD qualification could be obtained by purchase, and it seems more than likely that he studied at home, rather as an Open University student of today might do. He gained his MD in 1846 and, although he proudly listed this on his census return for 1851, he later dropped it from his list of qualifications, focussing instead on his chemical ones. By April of the same year he was installed, along with George Cook, as an overseer for the parish of St John.[15] Circumstantial though this evidence is, it does seem to point further to home, rather than foreign, study. By 1851, he had expanded into the less lovely world of the sewers and, in the census for that year, he gave his occupation as 'Dr Medicine Continental; Practical chemist and manure manufacturer'.

He ran his manufactory by emptying the cesspools of Hereford, using the contents for his manure, with a 'soil-yard' at the bottom of Aylestone Hill. His smelly factory was at one time the subject of legal proceedings for creating a nuisance, but the case was dropped. An instance, perhaps, of knowing the right people, for Andrew Rowan was a well-regarded and important member of the Woolhope Club, addressing it on several occasions with learned papers on a variety of topics.[16] There could hardly be a greater contrast between his hat-selling business, with its superior hats for the gentry of Hereford, his connection with Hereford's intelligentsia at the Woolhope Club and his nightly emptying of cess pits.

> **ROWAN'S PHOSPHORISED MANURE**
>
> HAVING been extensively used for the last four years, and highly approved of, by some of the leading Agriculturists of the Counties of Hereford and Monmouth, may be had on application to
>
> A. ROWAN, CHEMIST, BROAD-STREET,
>
> HEREFORD, or any of his AGENTS, who will furnish copies of testimonials.
> Mr. H. S. DUGGAN, Druggist, Broad-street, } HERE-
> Mr. W. WILLIAMS, Druggist, Bridge-street, } FORD.
> Mr. IRELAND, (Argus,) LEDBURY.
> Mr. GLOVER, Hatter, ROSS.
> Mr. COTTERELL, Corn-factor, ABERGAVENNY.
> Mr. RD. HALL, Druggist, High-street, BRECON.
> Mr. H. W. MORRIS, Druggist, KINGTON.
> Mr. CHAS. ALLEN, King's Arms, LEOMINSTER.
>
> Phosphorised Manure, cash, £6 per Ton in Hereford.
> Superphosphate of Lime, £7 10s. per Ton.

An advert in The Hereford Times
for 3 May 1850

He was also a regular contributor to the letters page of the *Hereford Times*. In February 1847, he wrote a lengthy scientific letter to the paper on the problems of potato disease, giving his own remedy for solving it, 'hoping that it may prove useful to the potato growing portion of the community'. He signed himself 'member of the Royal College of Chemistry, London'.[17] In December of the same year, he wrote two more long letters to the local paper about the need for the chemical analysis of soil in order to enhance crops.[18] A month later, he was back in print again on the same subject, in an argument with a clergyman about the fertility of subsoil – probably not a subject likely to excite the passions of many readers of the paper.[19] Despite gaining his medical qualifications, he was still a hat manufacturer, selling hats 'the bodies of which (being made with animal fur) ... resist the heaviest rain, and permit a free escape of perspiration without the necessity of artificial valves.'[20]

By April 1848, he had started yet another new line of business, informing the agriculturists of Herefordshire that he had commenced:

the manufacture of artificial manures, containing a rich supply of the alkaline and earthy phosphates, of which the soil of Herefordshire is generally deficient ... the article will be manufactured to meet the wants of the crops for which it is intended; and where a tonne or upwards is taken, an approximate analysis of the soil will be given in order to supply its deficiencies, as well as those of the plant.[21]

There speaks a true entrepreneur. He clearly became well known and respected by the agricultural community and, in October 1848, attended the annual dinner of the Abergavenny Farmers' Club. In the newspaper, with its account of prizes to long-serving servants, ploughing matches and prize-winning turnips, he was described as an 'agricultural chemist of Hereford'. In the same newspaper he had an advertisement for his latest venture which was the manufacture, 'with a new and improved apparatus of manures for the autumn planting of wheat, beans etc.'; he also sold a 'highly concentrated deodorising fluid, which acts instantaneously, fixing the most offensive exhalations in drains, cesspools etc.'[22]

At a meeting of the city council in February 1849, Andrew Rowan's application for exclusive rights to remove the city night-soil was granted, provided it was done at night and care was taken to ensure it did not drop into the streets.[23] It was done 'at an average cost of £1 per cesspool, with Andrew Rowan dealing with between 40 and 50 cesspools a year, using the contents to produce manure for farmers at his factory behind the Commercial Road gasworks.[24]

Despite his rather unpleasant night-time job, Andrew Rowan was clearly one of the city's worthies, and as such he was part of an enquiry into the poor state of street cleaning in the city. It was found that, because there had been increasing amounts of grit in the street sweepings, far less had been sold for manure. However, it was argued that if the grit could be separated from the other portion of the street sweepings, it would be desirable as an ingredient in builders' mortar. The committee had pleasure 'in stating that Mr A. Rowan, a practical chemist, as well as one of the most intelligent and useful members of the Board had suggested an inexpensive way of effecting this separation and was willing to superintend it himself. This was unanimously accepted.'[25]

In November of the same year, he wrote a rather cross letter to the *Hereford Times,* stating that he had planned to enter into the speculation of converting flax fibre into a marketable article, and had begun alterations to his premises at the Gas Works, when he received:

the unpleasant intelligence that a bill of indictment had been preferred ... for an alleged nuisance in manufacturing manure ... I have given up the speculation for the time, and probably forever in this city; for an unfavourable verdict would in all probability turn my attention to some favourable locality where I would not be likely to meet with the same annoyance that I have already experienced in carrying out my plans, which have already saved a considerable sum to the owners of property in the city, as well as conferred some benefit on the county.[26]

You can almost hear him mutter 'your loss, not mine'. However, he stayed in Hereford for, in March 1851, he gave evidence in a lengthy and complex case about the pollution or otherwise of a ditch in Ledbury and, in so doing, gave an interesting insight into his own professional and personal background when he said, under cross-examination:

I studied chemistry at the Royal College of Chemistry in London under Dr Hoffman: I was there as long I think as three months ... I was connected with it [chemistry] in the early part of my life with my father, who was a surgeon, an apothecary, and a practical chemist, living at Belfast; I was not regularly apprenticed to my father by indentures; I did not study chemistry as a profession at that time, but I have done so since; I have not, with the exception of Dr. Hoffman, studied under the direction of anyone, but I have for several years made it a matter of private study; I combine the trade of hatter with my chemical business ... I also have chemical works in which I manufacture artificial manure.[27]

Chemicals, and in particular, mercury were used in the hat-making business so it is not perhaps surprising that this versatile man had studied chemistry.

In April 1851, he was one of the signatories requesting that a public meeting be set up to take into consideration the best way of erecting an 'establishment of cheap baths, both common and medicated, with the Society for Aiding the Industrious'.[28] In May, he was part of a group reporting to the city commissioners on the price of gas, which he felt should be reduced.[29] In July he had contributed to a report by the committee appointed to enquire into the city wells and water carts, in which various recommendations were made for improvement. He was clearly a busy man.[30] Perhaps it was his extra-curricular activities, together with a thriving manure business that made him decide, in July of the same year, to advertise the sale of his hat manufacturing business.[31]

On Valentine's Day 1852, Andrew Rowan suffered a terrible blow. His wife Sarah died in her 38th year, along with an infant daughter, leaving Andrew Rowan and his other nine children to 'mourn her irreparable loss'.[32] These children ranged in age from a little over a year to 18 – no doubt the two eldest daughters would have found themselves in the role of mother to the younger children, as well as housekeeper and cook to their father. Despite this calamity, only two weeks later, Andrew Rowan, 'agricultural chemist', was again writing to the paper on one of his hobby horses, the growing of flax.[33] In May he was appointed city commissioner for St John's parish, another public office to add to his portfolio.[34] He was clearly a man who cared about the city and its people for, in June 1852, he was one of the signatories to a report on the generally defective system of drainage in the city.[35]

In March 1853, Andrew Rowan gave evidence at a rather bizarre trial, in which two gypsies were accused of poisoning a pig, which subsequently died. Andrew Rowan, in a change from gathering night soil, was given the entire contents of the pig's stomach for analysis. As the *Hereford Times* reported the case inaccurately, Andrew Rowan had to write yet another letter in which he stated that the substance was poisonous. There always seems to be a degree of confusion about Andrew Rowan's qualifications as, 'in reply to the question ... whether he was a member of the College of Physicians', he said that 'he was not practising as a physician but as a chemist, and that he was a member of the Royal College of Chemists'. The same edition of the paper carried the happy announcement that Andrew Rowan, M.D. of Harley Place had married Anne Lucy, youngest daughter of the late Charles William Drury, jeweller and silversmith, Banbury.[36] He was 45; his new wife, at the age of 29, was his junior by 16 years.

Not content with his hatting and manure business, by June 1854, Andrew Rowan was manager of the Herefordshire Coal and General Mercantile Company and, ever the entrepreneur, was, by October of the same year, advertising a reduction in the price of coal.[37] But, despite a new marriage and what appeared to be a thriving business life, there was also sadness for Andrew Rowan and his wife when, in February 1856, their son Charles died at the young age of seven months.[38] His manure factory continued to excite the hostility of people living nearby, engendering another charge of nuisance against him, causing him to defend himself robustly in print yet again.[39] He continued, however, to advertise his wares regularly in the local paper.

When he was in his early fifties he left Hereford, moving firstly to York, then to Scarborough where he seems to have added two more strings to an already rather fully strung bow. The *Scarborough Gazette* advertised his services regularly:

> A Rowan Homeopathic and Analytical Chemist, No 8 Queen Street Scarborough (opposite the post office) established for the preparation and sale of all homeopathic medicines, cocoa, chocolate and genuine teas. Medical galvanism practised. Soils, manures etc. analysed on moderate terms.[40]

The Victorians were fascinated by the study of galvanism, according to which it was believed that, if electricity was charged into the brain, a human corpse would come back to life for a short time. Quite what qualifications, if any, he had for this new service is unclear, but here he is again in 1864, still studying and passing examinations:[41]

Andrew Rowan was clearly a restless man, for he moved so regularly after he returned to Yorkshire that it is tempting to wonder what lay behind these frequent changes. By the time of the 1871 census the family were living in Barnsley. Under occupation he wrote 'M.D. Erlangen' as well as LSA London, LRCP Edinburgh, and LFPS Glasgow.[42] However, never one to ignore a new career opportunity, Andrew Rowan had also become a medical referee for the Royal Assurance Company.

By the time of the 1881 census the family had left Yorkshire and were living in Lewisham in a street of terraced houses. By this time Andrew Rowan simply stated, under occupation, that he was 'a medical practitioner'. The family neighbours were a mantle maker and a lodging housekeeper. Had the Rowan family perhaps come down in the world? There were two more moves, both in Lewisham, south London, before his death on 17 January 1891, in the 82nd year of his age.[43] He was clearly a man of many talents, a restless entrepreneur and, probably, both charming and charismatic. It is however possible, just possible, that he was also something of a fraud. George Eagle, the clairvoyant, admitted he was; Andrew Rowan probably never did.

The final character in this chapter, Robert Vaughan, was something of a slippery customer, at least about his age, as he never gave his correct age to the census enumerator.[44] The story of this man who, like Solomon Lazarus and Andrew Rowan, had several strings to his working bow,

Dr. Rowan, of Scarborough, late of Hereford, passed an examination at the faculty of Physicians and Surgeons of Glasgow, on Tuesday the 13th inst., and received their Diploma; and on Wednesday, the 14th inst., he also passed an examination at the Royal College of Physicians,

The Hereford Times *carried this notice on 17 September 1864* begins with the 1841 census. In this census, father and son, both named Robert Vaughan, were living in the same house in Gwynne Street, both working as coopers. Although this chapter concerns Robert Vaughan junior, his father plays a part in the following court case.

In April 1848, Robert Vaughan senior was the plaintiff in a case concerning trespass. The defendant was Mr Davies, a coach-builder, who had built a workshop on the banks of the Wye some 12 years earlier. However, Robert Vaughan complained that the windows overlooked his yard and premises and were the 'cause of much annoyance to his family'. He placed some boards and fencing near the windows; in return Mr Davies put his windows into another part of his workshop, again giving annoyance to Robert Vaughan. More boards were put up; Mr Davies had them knocked down. It was suggested that it was a pity that the court's time was to be taken up with so trifling an affair, but the parties were determined to slog it out in public. Robert Vaughan [junior] gave a lengthy deposition about the history of the said windows and the breaking of the boards. He said that he had lived with his father since 1843.[45] From about 1844, he had let out boats and found that the people who had hired them were frequently annoyed by the men in Mr Davies' workshop and that, to add insult to injury, Mr Davies had previously been up in court for 'throwing coal ashes upon my father and a young man named Trumper, almost smothering them'. Glimpses of both father and son as 'characters' certainly come through from the report of this case. At one point, the cross-examining lawyer caused much merriment 'by questioning the plaintiff as to his wearing of a moustache' and asking whether he had been 'an amateur actor, which latter he answered in the negative'.

The next witness was Ann Argest, who had worked as a charwoman for the Vaughan family for six years. She too had had 'a number of annoyances from the men employed by Mr Davies, which I am ashamed to explain'. She went on to say that a picture had been suspended from the workshop window, representing Robert Vaughan and his son on the gallows 'as large as life'.[46] Several witnesses were called to describe the buildings and the alleged damage done by the tearing down of the boards. The verdict was a mixed one, Vaughan senior winning on two counts and losing on one.[47]

From this point on, the spotlight falls on Robert Vaughan junior who, three months later, charged 'a very respectable young man, a mechanic' with assault. On the previous Thursday, a dance was taking place in a house where some of his tenants were living. One of his previous tenants, a woman, kept rapping on the shutter and calling for 'Prince Albert's March'. This was no doubt a reference to the moustache sported by Robert Vaughan, which had earned him the soubriquet 'Prince Albert', the said moustache no doubt aping that of Queen Victoria's husband. This so offended Robert Vaughan that he had the young woman taken into custody and charged with being a disorderly prostitute. The young mechanic was so incensed at this 'hammer to crack a nut' behaviour that he threatened to 'knock several holes in the complainant's head ... and to knock the hair off his face'. However this incident had a history – according to our respectable young mechanic, Robert Vaughan had, on a previous occasion, threatened him with a hammer; on another he had shot at him with a pistol and 'been guilty of many eccentricities'. Although it was the defendant who was ordered to keep the peace, Robert Vaughan does not emerge entirely innocent of aggressive behaviour in this account.[48]

In terms of court cases, a few peaceful years then passed but, in 1853, the *Hereford Journal*, under the heading of *The Beauties of English Law*, reported on a case in which Morgan Davies was charged with assaulting Robert Vaughan. Whether or not this was the same Mr Davies of the previous charge is not clear but it does sound suspiciously like a simmering feud. Davies was one of Vaughan's tenants who 'had permission to go down his yard to the river for water when the yard was open'. When Robert Vaughan asked him to make haste because he wanted to close the yard, Davies challenged him to a fight, saying he would 'put it into him rather sharpish'; he was joined by his wife, who also threatened to punch Vaughan. Both men claimed a right – Davies to his right of access to the river, Vaughan to his right to keep his yard locked at certain times. Vaughan sought permission to 'take the law into his own hands' but was told that 'neither of you has the right to take the law into your own hands, and commit a breach of the peace.' The case was then dismissed, and Robert Vaughan left the court complaining that 'what he was told he had no right to do was what he charged Davies with threatening to do, and which he sought to restrain him from doing.'[49]

Six years later, at the age of 47, this rather excitable character married. There is a posting on the internet which gives an intriguing insight into this marriage; according to this report, in 1859, Elizabeth Wilding married Robert Vaughan, a man some 20 or so years her senior. She was a sewing maid for whom Robert Vaughan, a confirmed bachelor, fell hook line and sinker.[50]

Married life seems to have calmed Robert Vaughan down, but there was one other incident of aggression when, in 1861, he was charged with using threatening language. He had, until just before this incident, been an assistant overseer for St John's parish. However, at a vestry meeting, his appointment had been revoked and Mr Austin Herbert, who had previously shared the role with him, was given sole responsibility. The new overseer had gone to collect payment of a rate from Robert Vaughan, who became 'exceedingly irritated' as he felt that Herbert had 'done him out of his place'. He told Herbert that, 'if it were in my power, you would not leave this house alive.' He then pulled off his coat and wanted to fight Herbert, who told the court he thought he was in bodily danger. Vaughan was bound over to keep the peace for 12 months, with a surety of £50.[51]

After this, Robert Vaughan seems to have turned his formidable energy into his role as a dancing teacher, where no doubt his moustache, if he still had it, would have cut a fine flourish. By 1871 Robert and his wife were both teachers of dancing and were parents to Arthur aged 10; Ada, 9; Edith, 5; Francis, 2 and Louisa 2 months.[52] By 1881 Elizabeth was no longer working, but bringing up those children who still remained at home, including three who had been born since the previous census: Percy, 9; Maude, 7 and Reginald, 4. Edith, now aged 15, had become a pupil dancing teacher. Sadly, there are no references to his classes or lessons in the local papers, but he could well have been a character akin to Mr Turveydrop, the dancing master in Charles Dickens' *Bleak House*. Perhaps Robert Vaughan too, like Prince Turveydrop, 'sometimes played the kit, dancing; sometimes played the piano, standing; sometimes hummed the tune with what little breath he could spare, while he set a pupil right.'[53] By the time of the 1891 census Robert Vaughan was still working as a dancing teacher. He died a few months later, presumably still in his dancing shoes. He seems to have been as confused about his age at the end of his life as when he was a young man for, in the census, he gave 77 as his age but on his death certificate in September of the same year, it was recorded that he was in fact 79.

This chapter has dealt with three men, all of them characters, but the final chapter will deal with two interesting women who both lived through revolution in distant countries, but who also lived in the parish, one as the wife of a dean, the other first as a child and then as an elderly woman.

7   The Slave Owner & the Governess

> In the midst of political upheaval and unrest, Frances maintained by her presence and force of personality a centre of stability on her plantations. Each year she arrived from the north for the autumn harvest, stayed through the winter, kept the accounts, paid the workers, negotiated contracts for the coming year, provided the seed for the next year's planting and returned to Philadelphia only when the heat, sand flies, fleas and snakes became too much to cope with.[1]

> I have often thought what an interesting kind of novel could be written from her life story – her mixed origins, her Quaker up-bringing, her life abroad, and her return to a quiet and increasingly lonely existence.[2]

Two of the most interesting people to come out of the research on parish characters were women: one, Frances Leigh, who lived through the American Civil War before coming to Hereford as a dean's wife; the other, Gertrude Dziewicki, daughter of a Polish Catholic father and a Quaker mother who spent her childhood in Hereford but her adult life as a governess in Poland in revolutionary times.

Frances Leigh was the daughter of the notable Herefordian actress, Fanny Kemble, and Pierce Butler, a wealthy slave owner. In 1832, Fanny had gone to America where she and Pierce met and fell in love. They married in 1834; it was a marriage of two volatile and strong-willed people who thrived, at least for a time, on the tensions between them. In the end, it was the fundamental difference towards the question of slavery – she was an abolitionist, he was not – that led, two daughters later, to a bitter divorce, in which Pierce Butler gained custody of the children, who both stayed in America.

When Pierce Butler died in 1867, two years after the abolition of slavery in America, his plantations passed into the hands of his daughter Frances who continued to run them. She provided child allowances for the children of workers and paid pensions for people too old to work, as well as opening a school for children in the day-time and for workers in the evening. When Frances met James Wentworth Leigh, her future husband, he recalled the fact that 'she managed, single-handed, her father's plantations, being all alone in the midst of Negroes, teaching and supplying their spiritual wants.'[3] The couple fell in love and, when Frances married Wentworth Leigh in 1871 she and her husband worked together on the plantation until they came to live in England in 1877, the plantation passing to another member of the Butler family. The couple moved to Hereford when Frances's husband was made dean of Hereford in 1894, remaining there for the rest of their lives.

There is no doubt that, by 21st-century attitudes and sensibilities, Frances was paternalistic, prejudiced and racist, arguing that, 'for the Negroes, I cannot help thinking that things are worse than they were when they were disciplined and controlled by a superior race.' Yet these uncomfortable views need to be taken in the context of the times in which she lived, 'for they were not markedly different from those of many persons who regarded themselves as liberal ... certainly they coincided with those of many an abolitionist.' What perhaps needs to be remembered is that, when slavery was abolished, 'it was difficult for both white landowner and former slave to work out a new relationship'.[4]

A delightful glimpse into life in the Leigh household at the end of the 19th century comes from a diary written in 1899 by a young American woman Ethel Dovey who, with her sister Alice, came to Hereford in order to take part in a *Café Chantant*[5] concert, a fund-raising event at the Shire Hall for the Lifeboat Association, which had been organised by Frances and her daughter. [6]

In this extract, Ethel describes the deanery as it was at the end of the 19th century, clearly a very comfortable middle class home. (The deanery was then at the east end of the Cathedral Close, in a building that is now part of the Cathedral School.) It was:

Dean Wentworth Leigh

Ethel and Alice Dovey

a beautiful old stone building opposite the beautiful cathedral … as we stop in front of the doorway, the large oak door is thrown wide open by a butler and the light streams out, and makes us all feel at home at once. We are all taken up to the beautiful drawing room where Mrs Leigh and her daughter [Alice] welcome us. A big fire burns in the handsome grate; a few candles are lighted, but the fire sends a soft light over the room.

After tea and muffins, the girls were shown to their bedroom where:

there is a large four-poster bed, with blue velvet hangings all the way round and a large blue satin comforter on the bed. At one side there is a lovely old fashioned oak chest of drawers and on the other is a big cosy blue armchair. There is a great blazing fire burning in the wide old grate and a soft fur rug is in front of it; two armchairs and a high-backed sofa with downy silk pillows heaped up on it … and a very handsome dressing table with two tall candles in silver sticks burning on each side.

There is much more in this vein, including musing on whether the deanery was haunted and on the relative merits of the two male guests at dinner – the curate was 'very nice' but of no interest to the sparky young girls, whereas Captain O'Brien 'was one of the handsomest men' they had seen; both girls fell in love with him but, alas, he was already spoken for as he was married. All the talk was about the forthcoming *Café Chantant* and, after dinner, they all went to the drawing room and sang and played pieces from the *Belle of New York*, *The Geisha* and *An Artist's Model*. These all refer to popular musical comedies of the period, stories of love gone wrong but, in the end, love gone right. There was a slightly risqué air about them, as this brief extract from *An Artist's Model* shows:

For lots of things we do you know
Are not precisely comme il faut
But that you'll find is often so
(chorus: in gay Bohemia).
The wild delights of days and nights
Would suit the chaste and luxurious taste
Of a Sultan or a Shah.
And this opinion still is rife,
You're bound to lead a shocking life,
Or bolt with someone else's wife,
In gay Bohemia.

There is something rather delightful about a dean, his wife and daughter singing these songs round the piano before going to see the girls, in their frothy dresses, at the *Café Chantant*. Their visit ended on a high note when Alice Leigh took the girls to the top of the cathedral tower, from where they looked down onto the Bishop's Palace and the Wye where 'tiny boats were lying lazily in the water and beautiful white swans swam to and fro, some with their heads under their wings asleep'.[7] It all sounds idyllic.

When Frances died in 1910, her English and American friends paid for a stained glass window in her memory to be installed in the cathedral. Although she was an apologist for slavery, Frances was nevertheless loved by her ex-slaves and, in the window; this is reflected in the image of a black child who peeps over the shoulder of St Francesca.

Frances Leigh window, Hereford Cathedral

Frances has another memorial in the form of a book she wrote. *Ten Years on a Georgia Plantation Since the War* described her life in the deep south. Gertrude Dziewicki also wrote a book. Hers was about her life in Poland. In addition, she wrote hundreds of letters about her life as a governess to her aunt Annie in Hereford.

Gertrude Elizabeth Dziewicki was born and brought up in Hereford, but she led a more than ordinary life as a governess and private tutor in Eastern Europe in the late 19th century.[8] Her story includes the expulsion from Poland of a political émigré, a stormy marriage, her husband's death by drowning, glimpses of aristocratic life, revolution in fin de siècle Poland and, finally, burial in the wrong grave.

In 1871, when Gertrude first appeared in the census, she was living with her Quaker aunt and uncle (sister and brother) at 10 Broad Street.[9] Joseph Jones was a bookseller and Annie, who never married, was a dealer in fancy articles and her brother's housekeeper. Jane Jones, another sister who was three years older than Joseph, was born in St John's parish on 8 April 1826. She was to become Gertrude's mother.

Nothing is known of Jane's childhood and the first glimpse of her comes from her mother's 1848 diary, written when Jane was already a teacher. It is clear from the diary that Mrs Jones was in a state of great depression and anxiety about her daughter. Whilst teaching in Bridgwater in Somerset, Jane had met and fallen in love with a charismatic Polish émigré, Severin Dziewicki. He came from a cultured, but relatively impoverished, background. On leaving school in 1828 he went to study law and literature at the University of Warsaw. Revolution, however, interfered with his studies and he left university early in order to join the Polish army, taking part in the November Revolution, the Polish revolt against Russia in 1830. After its failure, he was one of the many young Polish political émigrés who were forced to flee Poland. He arrived in England in 1835 where he settled, eventually becoming a teacher of French and classics.

Severin had been in England for over ten years when he met and fell in love with Jane Jones, the young Quaker from Hereford.[10] It was clearly a genuine love match for the couple, but that was not how Jane's parents viewed it. They were horrified by the prospect

Joseph and Annie Jones, Jane's uncle and aunt who lived at 10 Broad Street

of their Quaker daughter marrying a man who was not only 16 years her senior, but also a Catholic and a foreigner, and they strenuously opposed the match. The stubborn couple, however, were married at Saint Nicholas Church (St John's was closed for marriages at the time owing to the cathedral restorations) on 29 December 1849. On the day of the marriage 'only one sister arrived … to represent the family at the marriage. This was followed by the wedding breakfast at which other members appeared, but their silent and gloomy attitude made it feel more like a funeral … in vain the vicar[11] talked and joked, but not a smile, not even a good wish to begin a new life!'[12]

It would seem that the parents' worries for their daughter's marriage were not ill-founded and clues for this emerge from the notes that Henry, Severin's eldest son, wrote about his father many years later:

Jane Dziewicki in 1858

> He was an extraordinarily versatile man, reading Latin poets, writing poetry (Polish of course), making friends with all the cultured professors he came into contact with, making electrical machines and giving us shocks with Leyden jars; an expert in foreign cookery, in gardening, in brewing, in raising tomatoes … and so on and so on. He had a taste for pretty well everything, except saving money. Had he had *that* (for I know he earned a great deal by his lessons) things might have turned out very differently for all of us. But he liked to swank … he certainly had great talents of making himself liked by everybody, and loved by some. Mother and he quarrelled sometimes, I know, but they made it up directly. Mother was enormously under his influence, it was almost magnetic.[13]

Severin Dziewicki from an undated carte de visite

Severin also, it seems, had a taste for drink as, in the family papers, there are pencil notes by an anonymous writer that say, 'Severin D's intemperate habits <u>must</u> be mentioned'. Someone else has written a bold NO.[14]

After their marriage, the Dziewickis continued working in Bridgwater for a while and their eldest son, Henry was born there in March 1851. By July of the same year the family was back in Hereford and Jane Dziewicki was advertising the fact that she had taken over a boarding and day school for young ladies in Wye Bridge Street. It must have been hard work for her – moving back to Hereford, looking after a small baby and running a school – but Jane was at pains to assure parents and guardians that she had been engaged in tuition for several years, and that her chief aim was 'to combine the intellectual improvement with the domestic comfort of her pupils'. In the same advertisement Severin begged 'to inform the Nobility, Clergy, Gentry, and the Public in general of this City and County that he gave private lessons in families and schools in the French, German, Greek and Latin languages, and in mathematics. He was able to provide high testimonials as to character and abilities from Noblemen, Clergymen, and Gentlemen whose children he had instructed.'[15]

By June 1852, Severin was employed as a professor of modern languages at Hereford Cathedral School, whilst also seeking to supplement his income by 'giving instruction to young men during their vacation'.[16] He clearly stayed at the school for several years, as he was still there in July 1861 and he sounded, at that time, to be as hard-working as his wife. Severin was always at pains to describe himself as 'Monsieur S.B. de Dziewicki, lieutenant in the late Polish Army' and it is likely that he would have cut a somewhat exotic and dashing figure in Hereford. On 21 February 1854, a month after his second son Theodore was born, he advertised the fact that he was going to give a morning lecture, free of charge, at the Green Dragon Hotel on 'the most interesting events of the late Hungarian war, and the present aggression of Russia, together with her position as regards other European countries.'[17] There was a 'numerous and respectable audience' for what was clearly a passionate lecture, deeply hostile to Russia. The report in the *Hereford Times* ran to well over two columns and strong meat it was. In his talk, Severin thundered on and on to regular smatterings of applause and, less frequently, laughter. Finally, the lecturer retired amid applause. There must also have been sighs of relief, but perhaps audiences in those days were made of sterner stuff.[18]

By 1856, the family was living at the idyllic-sounding Rose Cottage on Aylestone Hill, spending six years there, the longest they seem to have settled anywhere. Many years later, Theodore asked: 'How could we forget Rose Cottage, with its honeysuckle porch, green lawn, and beautiful apple trees, loaded with fruits? It seems to me like a dream of Paradise.'[19] The couple's next two children, Mary and Joseph (known as Roman), were both born there, Mary in 1856 and Joseph in 1858. Theodore wrote a tender comment about Joseph's birth, recalling that 'papa made us go upstairs to see him, and we opened his tiny hands, which he always would shut up again.'[20] It sounded a happy time for all the family, and Jane even seems to have had a well-earned break from running a school. It was not to last since, by April 1861, still with four children under ten to care for, Jane had moved her day and boarding school to 3 Elizabeth Place, Portland Street, Hereford

Houses in Elizabeth Place, Portland Street, Hereford. No.3 has the yellow door

where the family lived on site and it was here that Gertrude, the couple's youngest child, was born four months later.

By July 1862, Severin was advertising the sale by auction of all his household furniture and effects.[21] No reason was given but perhaps his swanking and intemperate habits had finally got the upper hand and, from subsequent events, he might have been suffering from depression. It seems that, soon after this advertisement, he had moved from the Portland Street house to one in Tenbury, where his work seems to have taken him, although whether he was alone or with his family is not clear. On 15 December, he had travelled alone from Tenbury to Leominster to seek lodgings there as they would have been more central for his work. He never returned home, for he drowned in the river Lugg in Leominster. He was only 49. On the evening of his death, he had gone into the refreshment room of the station where his behaviour seems to have been a little strange. Mary Bowdley, who kept the refreshment room, testified that:

> on the evening in question he came into the [refreshment] room three different times in the evening, the last time being about half past six o'clock; he had one glass of ale between five and six o'clock ... that was all he had, and he asked me how long the train would be; I said, 'for Woofferton?' he said 'yes'; 'about an hour', I replied; after I had drawn the glass of ale I observed that he was tipsy; he was not tipsy before he had the glass of ale; he missed the train and there was not another until eight o'clock; he said nothing about walking home; no train would take him to Tenbury that night.

According to the Bradshaw timetable, the train to Woofferton would have left Leominster at 5.50pm, when Severin was, apparently, at the station.[22] He left the station at around 6.30pm. His watch stopped at 6.50pm, so he must have drowned very soon after his departure, yet nine days passed before his body was found on Christmas Eve. What an appalling Christmas that must have been for the family. The police superintendent who subsequently examined the bridge found marks of mud on it, as though someone had either slipped off or tried to scramble back. When asked, Jane's brother, Joseph, said that he 'considered the deceased a very unlikely man to do away with himself'. The coroner also considered that the death was 'accidental ... [the jury] had heard of the state in which he was, that he was too late for the train, and that his body had been found in the river on the nearest way to his home, and there was evidence to suggest that he was in good circumstances.' However, there was also a feeling in Joseph's deposition that Severin was deeply unsettled, for he commented that Severin 'used to travel about ... we have known him the worse for liquor, but since he has been at Tenbury he has been steady ... improving his means and getting on well.'[23]

Was it suicide or accident? The jury at his inquest concluded that the death was accidental, but, since suicide was a crime at the time and this would have been a well-regarded family, despite Severin's intemperate habits, perhaps this was a deliberate act of kindness. Neither the jury nor the coroner seem to have considered the apparently deliberate missing of the train, or the fact that a tipsy Severin had set out in the dark of a winter night to walk the ten miles home, a puzzle. Was he, in fact, in such a melancholy and suicidal frame of mind that, having finally plucked up his courage with the help of some ale, he wove an unsteady path to the river bridge and plunged to his certain death? He could not swim, the current there was strong, the river high and bitterly cold – so death was certain.

Severin was buried in the churchyard of Leominster Priory, a proud man even in death, for on his tomb is written:

> Lieut. SEVERIN BOLISLAS de DZIEWICKI,
> of the Polish Army 1831-2, one of the ten students
> who took the historical Arsenal from the Russians.
> A Freemason initiated at Dijon, France,
> A Poet Literate & Classical Scholar,
> Master of seven languages,
> was drowned in the Lugg at Leominster,
> Dec 15th 1862.[24]

His tombstone seems to have disappeared during the re-ordering of the churchyard, but it appears as number 191 on the churchyard map.[25]

After their father's death, the four eldest Dziewicki children were sent to Catholic seminaries in France for their education. Henry was 12, Theodore 10 and Roman 7. Mary was sent, at the age of 9, to a French Catholic convent near Boulogne. This odd situation, given that the family were staunch Quakers, came about as the family had got to know, because of their shared Polish and Catholic connections, the Catholic Bodenhams of Rotherwas. In 1850 Charles Bodenham had married the Polish aristocrat Irene Marie Morwska who, when Severin Dziewicki died, 'regarded it as her patriotic and religious duty to rescue the children of her late countryman from the dangers of heresy'.[26]

The children must have been bewildered and homesick, yet they also had the British stiff upper lip in abundance. Their father had died; they had been removed from the care of their mother and sent to a country where they did not know the language and where Catholicism

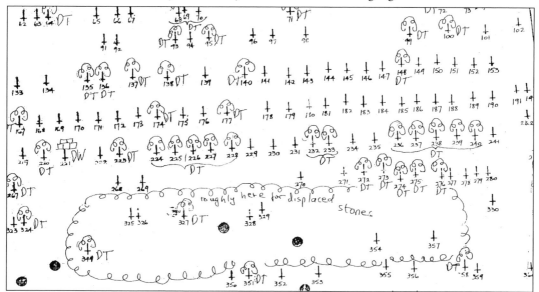

Part of a plan drawn in 1991 (not to scale) showing the layout of graves in the churchyard to the south-east of Leominster Priory. Severin Dziewicki's grave is number 191; the black circles indicate the position of trees.

rather than Quakerism was the order of the day. Yet, in the few surviving letters from the boys, alongside homesickness, determination to succeed shines through. Sadly, Theodore died when only 16 but, on leaving school, none of the other children returned to live in England. Henry, the eldest, became a Catholic and a lecturer at Krakow University; Joseph became a sheep shearer in Australia and died from a haemorrhage of the lungs when he was only 38; whilst Mary became a governess in Poland.[27]

Gertrude was only one year old when her father died; shortly after that her siblings disappeared abroad. Quite why and when Jane left Gertrude with her brother and sister is unclear but she seems to have followed her other children to France. Gertrude must have felt bewildered and abandoned, although Aunt Annie was, she wrote, kind but strict. She was the only one of the children to have a Quaker education, although her schooling began in non-Quaker schools

Henry (standing) and Theodore c.1860

in Hereford. The only satisfactory one of these was 'run by a lady of ancient family ... Miss Pye gave all her time to us, so that was an epoch that left a sweet memory ... we had, too, an artist for Drawing and Painting, Mr Oldmeadow. He was quite perfectly charming: the way he taught absolutely enchanting.'[28]

Although it was unusual for children whose parents were not both Quakers to be accepted at a Quaker School, Gertrude was sent to Sidcot School in Winscombe, north Somerset, when she was 13, leaving there when she was 15.[29] Gertrude liked to think of herself as something of an artist, and a piece of her art survives in a book compiled for the General Meeting of the school in 1876.[30]

On leaving school, Gertrude trained as a teacher. By 1880 she was working at Mrs Smith's kindergarten and advance school at 21 Richmond Terrace, Bristol.

Gertrude's teaching life in England was, however, a short one as, in 1886, she and her sister Mary set off for Poland where they were to work as governesses. Virtually

An example of Gertrude's art from her school book

*Above: Gertrude as a young teacher (seated
bottom left), teachers and pupils c.1882
Left: Gertrude in Hereford in 1882 aged 20*

nothing is known of Mary's life there ,but Gertrude stayed in Poland, with two years in Russia, until the outbreak of the First World War. Throughout her time there, she wrote hundreds of letters to her aunt Annie in England. When she and her sister set out on their adventures, Poland was a divided country, with great swathes 'belonging' to Russia, Prussia and the Austrian empire. Nineteen years later, Gertrude lived through the Polish attempt to shake off these foreign masters, with her letters home dealing with the everyday, such as having a new carpet in her room, to the riot and revolution on the streets of Warsaw where she was living.

On arriving in Poland, the sisters went first to Krakow, where their brother Henry was a lecturer in English at the university. Gertrude was clearly enchanted by being 'abroad'. She quickly decided that she liked foreign gentlemen who took off their hats with a grand sweep and who kissed her hand – very un-English, very un-Quakerly. In October 1886, after only two weeks with her 'new' family in Krakow, Gertrude left her brother's home in order to start her work as a governess in Kanie, a few hours from Lublin. She was to teach the children of Princess Woroniecka, the relative of the Polish member of the Bodenham family who had organised the schooling of Gertrude's siblings several years earlier.[31]

Kanie, with its remoteness, appalling roads, secret masses and political tensions, must have seemed very strange to the Quakerly Gertrude but she, in her turn, seemed very odd to the people she met, for she 'was stared at by the servants & peasants as if I was some sort of extraordinary specimen escaped from the zoo. At first I found it a little embarrassing but am getting more accustomed to it.' After what must have been a fairly frugal life in her Quaker home in Hereford, life with the Polish aristocracy, in the days before many of them lost all they had during revolutionary upheavals in the following century, must have seemed very grand, and

Gertrude in 1896

Gertrude enjoyed, albeit as a governess rather than as an equal, something of Polish aristocratic society.

Yet, despite the excitement of life at Kanie, with its regular shoals of visitors, depression and loneliness sometimes crept into Gertrude's cheerful letters to her aunt. The work itself was hard and unremitting, so much so that, at times, her bones ached dreadfully and her head was like lead. Although Gertrude appears to have made friends, her social life, such as it was, is rarely mentioned, although she did occasionally have picnics and outings with other English people. Mr Holloway was often referred to in Gertrude's letters and her aunt was curious enough to ask Gertrude about him, possibly sensing a romance. However, Gertrude merely wrote:

you asked me who Mr Holloway was ... he is a clerk in the Indo-Telegraph office – very well-educated, rather heavy but a downright good fellow ... he's been very kind in lending me English papers (not books) that come to the office but you must not think I am alone in this respect for he treats all the English damsels of his acquaintance the same.

Homesickness was also a problem and it is clear that Gertrude yearned for England. Only a year after her arrival in Kanie, she wrote:

how glad I shall be when I am back in England again ... however I suppose this is my place as I am here but it is very hard to feel contented ... I think it is much nicer to live in a small house in England where everything is civilised ... on Wednesday the *Hereford Times* came. I was so delighted to have it.[32]

There are many gaps in her letters but she seems to have worked as a governess for several years for various families in both Poland and Russia, but by February 1905, she was back in Warsaw and watching the charmed life of the Polish aristocracy unravel, as mayhem and revolution overturned the old order of things. It is her letters during this period that are the most interesting ones in the archive.[33] In February 1905, she wrote to her aunt:

> it is just two weeks since the strikes began ... the university is closed & so the students will go abroad to study but some may stay here because they are known to be such revolutionists. At the great meeting they held in their hall they tore down the Czar's picture, & poked it into the stove amid great shouts. Some of the Russian professors feebly remonstrated but no-one paid the least heed to them. The adventures they are having in all the gymnasiums now would fill volumes. There is no getting any sort of order as the boys & girls just simply refuse to study in Russian. At one large school the other day one of the head girls presented a petition to the Director which he immediately flung to the ground. In an instant every class was in an uproar, & the girls, about a hundred of them, crowded round the man, abusing him right & left & those nearest scratching & clawing him. However, he managed to get to the telephone to communicate to the police. Meantime a lot of students came in to help increase the row & when the police appeared the stampede & confusion were truly awful.

By May she was writing:

> I was waiting every day to tell you how things have passed off in this dreadful week ... Monday being the 1st and the day of all the Socialist demonstrations all the shops were closed & everybody forbidden to work ... Warsaw is quite in the hands of the police & the workmen now. So all day the streets on our side of the town were very quiet but fighting began at about 2 p.m. on account of one of the socialist workmen firing on the soldiers, the latter having commanded the red flags of liberty to be lowered. About fifty were killed & many wounded ... it was such superbly fine weather & to think of such cruel slaughtering going on quite near! Then in the evening the crowd got exasperated with the Cossacks & a bomb was thrown – it was a horrible shock. I jumped & was unnerved & could not keep myself from crying – the rarest thing in the world with me. All the windows where it was thrown were simply taken out as cleanly as if they had never been put in. The bomb was heard all over the greater part of the city & a horse's head was thrown up on the roof of a house. Three Cossacks were killed at once & one was wounded. All the victims were buried in the dead of the night.

Not surprisingly, when Aunt Annie received these letters in Hereford, she encouraged Gertrude to return to England but, despite the unrest, Gertrude was unwilling to leave. It is not clear from her letters how well (if at all) she spoke Polish, but, by this time, she had come to love Poland.[34] She wrote that as I 'still have work to do & am not much affected by all these strikes it is best to remain ... I am sure I will always live here & I do so love it for I have made many good friends here & I have a great sympathy for my father's race especially now when such tremendous efforts are being made for freedom.'

By 1907 Gertrude wrote that she had been considering returning to England but 'it is a very serious question as of course it always means making a fresh start in my life & as I am

Gertrude in 1929

no longer young I have not the energy of former years.' But such a fresh start was not yet to be, and Gertrude remained in Poland, doing her best to make ends meet with her teaching until the outbreak of the First World War, when she had a very frightening journey back to England. She was in Danzig (now Gdansk) when war broke out and wrote that 'each day grew more threatening – bulletins everywhere, at every street corner, & in many shop windows. Still people hoped against hope that the worst would be staved off. But Friday evening the news came & all the church bells began to toll.'

It took Gertrude some effort to get out of Poland but eventually, after many adventures, she arrived back in Hereford 'a washed out wreck'.[35]

Gertrude appears to have settled back into life in Hereford where she took up a teaching post, but, as she no longer needed to write letters to her aunt, there are only fragments to help piece together the rest of her life here.

By the 1940s Gertrude had become frail, deaf and eccentric. Her immediate family had either died or were living in Poland but, in what must have been an increasingly lonely old age, she did have her cats. Gertrude had been attending Quaker meetings and Richard Smith, the secretary of the Quakers in Hereford, appears to have taken responsibility for her welfare: most of what is known of the elderly Gertrude comes from his letters to Gertrude's cousin, John Sturge Stephens. By December 1944 her living room was:

> in a deplorable position. I have suggested having it cleared & all unnecessary things disposed of so that she could move into it & have sunshine & also her bed in the middle of the room ... but she will do nothing. Her bedroom is quite unfit for anyone to see, things, including treasury notes have fallen down under the bed, but she will allow no-one to get anything out.

It was not only the squalor in which she lived, but also her financial situation which was a worry, as the increasingly frantic letters from Richard Smith to John Sturge Stephens show. In 1944 he wrote:

> I am so worried about Gertrude Dziewicki that I feel I must write about her financial position which she seems to take so lightly. I have tried to talk to her but she just says 'I cannot be rushed'. I have tried writing a note showing that she is spending more than she receives & urging her to reconsider the question of applying for the Old Age Pension, but she has not replied ... it is clear that she needs at least £2 a week but I have been careful because she is liable to use it for purposes other than her support. For instance, she told me some time ago that she sent £1 to South Africa for feeding cats as a result of meeting two ladies ... her general health is good, but she has been in bed for so long that her power of walking is naturally getting less ... I am sorry to write at such length, but I do not feel that I can bear the responsibility alone.[36]

A few months later, his worries were resolved for, in early January 1945, Gertrude went into the Social Welfare Institution, a home in Ledbury. Although, by 1930, it had become a public assistance institution, this 'home' was originally built as the Ledbury workhouse and, with the title of 'institution', it must still have had shades of the workhouse about it. Her admission sounds as though it might well have been an emergency one, as Richard Smith says that the cost of the ambulance was 22s 6d. He was anxious about Gertrude's welfare and wrote that he would 'endeavour to run over if I find that my petrol allowance will permit'. He was also concerned that she had 'everything she requires such as chocolates and sweets'.[37]

It was clear, from various letters at the time, that her mind was also rather confused but perhaps, in the conditions in which she found herself, a frailty of mind was a blessing. In 1946 C.S. Smith, the Master at the Social Welfare Institution,[38] wrote to John Sturge Stephens explaining that Gertrude refused to sign some legal documents relating to her affairs 'on the grounds that she must see Mary first [her sister long dead]. Her mind not being normal and wandering it is very difficult to deal with, & I am therefore returning the documents unsigned.' By November 1947 she had a heart attack but she lingered on until she died after a slight stroke at the end of 1948. Complications seemed to beset Gertrude after her death, for her sole executor, a solicitor at Symonds and Spencer in Hereford, had pre-deceased her, leaving the residual legatees having to take out letters of administration.[39]

Gertrude had wanted to be interred with her mother but, in an ironic twist of fate, even her final laying to rest had elements of the bizarre about it. Again Mr Smith was involved, for in June 1949 he wrote to John Sturge Stephens that:

> when we searched the records for the grave of Gertrude's mother, the sheet was in such bad condition that it seemed impossible to locate it. Then the deputy-superintendent said it was 519A in the old All Saints ground. Gertrude was duly buried there ... a few days ago I was walking down one of the paths & was surprised to find a stone marked *Jane de Dziewicki* with date of death 1902 and the names of two sons ... I saw the deputy-super-intendent & we again went through the records. We found the name but it was number 519A in St Nicholas ground.[40]

The letter went on to discuss the removal of the coffin but Home Office permission was needed and Mr Smith was 'advised to leave things as they are and keep the matter a secret'. However her cousin John was appalled and it was decided that permission would be sought to have Gertrude buried with her mother. After much legal shenanigans involving the Home Office, on 31 August 1949, a letter went to the Town Clerk of Hereford saying that a licence would be granted subject to the following conditions:

> That the removal be effected with due care and attention to decency, early in the morning.
> That freshly made ground lime be freely sprinkled over the coffin, the soil, or any matter that be offensive.
> That the remains be forthwith re-interred in another grave in the Burial Ground, Hereford.[41]

And so, at 8am on 24 September 1949, with just the Quaker Mr Smith representing the family, Gertrude was finally laid to rest with her mother. The tombstone reads as follows:

In loving memory
of
JANE DE DZIEWICKA
née Jones
who died May 13th 1902.
Also of her sons
THEODORE
and
ROMAN.
'To die is gain
I will give thee rest.'
GERTRUDE ELIZABETH
DZIEWICKA
who died 30th Dec. 1948
aged 87 years.[42]

How sad it is to imagine the intelligent, cultured Gertrude, who had been governess to a Princess' children in Poland and lived through revolution, ending her days in what was little more than an institution and then being re-buried a little after dawn with only one witness. But, sad though her later life was, she has, in her letters, left behind the sense of a lively woman who lived and worked in Eastern Europe in interesting times and who had a 'life well lived'.

Gertrude's tombstone in Hereford Cemetery

Epilogue

I began this research soon after I moved to Hereford, knowing nothing about the parish or its 'church'. It has taken several years of poring over archives, analysing census returns and hunting down stories in newspapers. It has been a fascinating journey and one that could have continued as I sought out just one more fact, or researched yet another name from the census. However, I reached a point when I felt that I had what I hoped was an interesting story and decided to stop before the interesting became tedious. Readers of this book may well have more information on aspects of the material included and I would always be happy to hear from people who want to add to the stories told here.

When I walk around the parish streets now, I can people them with 'characters' from the past: the many labourers who worked for a pittance, the canons and their staff, the women who died young in childbirth, the respectable shop-keepers, the odd and the eccentric. I sometimes come to with something of a start when I realise I am in the 21st century, and not the medieval or the Victorian periods.

I hope that, as a reader, you will sense the ghosts of the parishioners of St John's as you go about your 21st century business in the streets around the cathedral that made up, for a thousand years or more, the parish that disappeared.

APPENDIX LIST OF PARISH VICARS

This gives as comprehensive a list of parish vicars as can be made. Start and end dates are often unknown as the only dates available are those that appear in records for a specific event.

Name	Role	Date	Source
William	canon and chaplain	13th century	HCA 494
De Leominster, Walter	clerk	1316	HCA 63
Hanewelle, Robert de	perpetual vicar	1333	HCA 1879
Credenhill, William	chaplain/vicar	1363	HCA 1014, 70
Baker, John alias Salwarpe	vicar	1386	Gilbert[1], Trefnant[2]
Robert	perpetual vicar	1333/4	HCA 43
Bradley, William Brother	vicar	1407	HCA 1154
Maxey, William	vicar Putley/Vowhurch	1423/24, 1445	HCA 184, Spofford[3]
Rogers, Roger	chaplain	1444	HCA 3204
Lynke, John	vicar	1457	Stanbury[4]
Brystow, Thomas	curate/vicar St Peter	1522/1527	HCA 7031/1 fol 32r 8 July 1522 and fol 40r 24 June 1527
Skynner, Philip	vicar	1588(?)-1609	Havergal[5]
Baughan, John	succentor, vicar	1604-29	HCA 2353, Havergal[6]
Jones, Evan	custos 1629, vicar Putley, Vowchurch	1609-37	Havergal[7]
Dryden, Jonathan (Bryden)	vicar	1636	Sacks 19/349
Peyton, William	vicar and chaplain of New College	1635-79	Havergal[8]
Gwillim, Thomas	vicar	1687- resigned 1706	HCA 7003/4/3 no. 15
Crowther, William	vicar	1713-66	HCA 7003/4/3 no.36
Guest, Joseph	vicar	1766-82 resigns	HCA 7003/4/4 no.56
Underwood, Richard	vicar	1782-1819	HCA 7003/4/4 no.63
Garbett, James	vicar	1819-resigned 1840	HCA 7003/4/4 no.80
Hanbury, John	vicar, rector St Nicolas	1840-59	HCA 7003/4/4 no.99
Goss, John	vicar, subchanter 1862, custos 1873	1853 -77 death	Havergal[9]
Capel, Alfred	vicar	1877-1917 death	Havergal[10]

BIBLIOGRAPHY

Abbreviations

CRO   Cornwall Record Office
HAS   Hereford Archive service
HCA   Hereford cathedral archives
HJ   Hereford Journal
HT   Hereford Times
Sacks   This refers Manuscripts of the Corporation of Hereford, also known as the 'Sack books' as these records were, for centuries, stored in sheepskin sacks
TWNFC   *Transactions of the Woolhope Naturalists Field Club*

Articles in magazines
Barrett, P., 'Hereford cathedral in the 19th century', *Friends of Hereford Cathedral annual report, 1986*
Breyer, Betty, An American in Hereford, 2003, *Cantilupe Journal, no 2, Autumn 2003*
Capes, W.W., The vicarage of St John the Baptist, *Diocesan Messenger 1915*
Jancey, E.M., 'Hereford cathedral and the parish of St John the Baptist' *The Friends of Hereford cathedral annual report 1984*
Morrill, Sylvia A., 'Poor Law in Hereford 1836-1851', *TWNFC*, 1974, vol. XLI
Waysblum, M., 'The Catholic Boys at Ackworth: from letters before and after their time there,' *Journal of the Friends Historical Society, vol 44, 1952*

Books
Aylmer, G. and Tiller, J., *Hereford Cathedral, a history*, 2000
Bannister, A.T., *The register of Thomas Spofford, Bishop of Hereford 1422-1448*, 1917
     The register of Richard Mayew Bishop of Hereford 1504-1516, 1919
     The register of Charles Bothe, Bishop of Hereford 1516-1535, 1921
     Diocese of Hereford Institutions 1539-1900, 1923
     The cathedral church of Hereford, its history and constitution, 1924
Barrett, P., *The College of Vicars Choral at Hereford cathedral*, 1980
Barrow, J., *The canons and citizens of Hereford c.1160-c.1240*, 1999
Barrow, J.S., *Fasti ecclesiae Anglicanae 1066-1300*, vol.8, 2002
Boucher, C., et al., *Death in the Close, a medieval mystery*, 2015
Branson, T. and Eisel, J. *Herefordshire clockmakers and watchmakers*, 2005
Britton, John, *The history and antiquities of the cathedral church of Hereford*, 1831
Bryson, Bill, *At Home*, 2010
Burke, Sir Bernard, *Genealogical and Heraldic Dictionary of the Peerage and Baronetcy*, 42nd edition, 1880
Burrow, E.J., *Hereford Illustrated*, 1897
Capes, W.W. (ed.), *The register of John Trefnant, Bishop of Hereford 1389-1404*, 1914
Cressy, D., *Birth, marriage and death: ritual, religion, and the life-cycle in Tudor and Stuart England*, 1999

Cross, J.L. and Livingstone, E.A. (eds), *The Oxford dictionary of the Christian church*, 2005

Dickens, Charles, *Bleak House*, 1853

Dohar, W.J., *The Black Death and pastoral leadership, the diocese of Hereford in the 14th century*, 1995

Duffy, Eamon, *The Stripping of the Altars*, 1992

Duncumb, J., *Collections towards the history and antiquities of the county of Hereford*, vol.1, 1804

Dziewicki, G., *Glimpses of Polish Life in Town and Country Pre-War to 1914*, 1937

Eales-White, J.C., *Records of Hereford cathedral school*, 1931

Edwards, Kathleen, *The English secular cathedrals in the Middle Ages*, 1967

Firth, C.H., *Acts and ordinances of the Interregnum, 1642-1660*, 1911, pp.840-84

Griffiths, R.G., *The register of Thomas de Cantilupe, 1275-1282*

Havergal, F., *Fasti herefordenses & other antiquarian memorials of Hereford*, 1869

Horn, J.M., revised Lepine, D., *Hereford Diocese, Fasti ecclesiae Anglicanae 1300-1541*, 2009

Humfrys, W.J., *Memories of old Hereford*, 1924

Johnson, R., *The ancient customs of the City of Hereford*, 1882

Klausner, D.N. (ed.), *Records of early English drama, Herefordshire and Worcestershire*, 1990

Lascelles & Co., *Directory and Gazetteer of Hereford 1851*

Lehmberg, S., *Cathedrals under siege: cathedrals in English society, 1600-1770*, 1996
    The reformation of cathedrals: cathedrals in English society, 1485-1603, 1988

Leigh, F., *Ten years on a Georgia plantation since the war*, 1883

Lepine, D., *A brotherhood of canons serving God*, 1995
    'Ande all our paresshens': secular cathedrals and parish churches in late medieval England, 2006

Lobel, Mary D. (ed.), Historic towns – maps and plans of towns and cities in the British Isles, vol. 1, 1969

Marshall, G., *The shrine of St Thomas de Cantilupe in Hereford cathedral*, 1930
    Hereford cathedral, its evolution and growth, c.1951

Matthews, Frederick, *Fragments and fancies*, 2011

Moorman, John, *A history of the Church in England*, 1973

Parry, J.H., (ed.), *The register of John de Trilleck 1344-1361*, 1910
    The Register of John Gilbert Bishop of Hereford (1375-1389), 1913
    (ed.), *The register of Robert Mascall, Bishop of Hereford (1404-1416)*, 1916
    The Register of John Stanbury, Bishop of Hereford (1453-1474), 1918

Pearn, A.M., 'Origin and Development of urban churches and parishes: a comparative study of Hereford, Shrewsbury and Chester', 1988 (*D. Phil thesis*)

Powell, J., *Hard times in Herefordshire, the effects of the workhouse and the New Poor Law*, 2008

Pym, Barbara, *No fond return of love*, 1961

Rees, W.J., *The Hereford Guide*, 1806

Roberts, G., *The shaping of modern Hereford*, 2001

Ross, D., *Royalist, but ... Herefordshire in the English Civil War 1640-51*, 2012

Setterfield. Diane, *The Thirteenth Tale*, 2006

Shoesmith, R., *The Civil War in Hereford*, 1995

Smith, L.T. (ed.), T*he Itinerary of John Leland in or about the years 1535-1543* parts IX, X and XI, 1910

Smyth, Charles, *Cyril Forster Garbett, Archbishop of York*, 1959

Stone, R. and Appleton-Fox, N., *A view from Hereford's past: a report on the archaeological excavation in Hereford cathedral Close in 1993*, 1996

Tarlow, S., *Ritual, belief and the dead in early modern Britain and Ireland*, 2011

Tate, W.E., *The parish chest: a study of the records of parochial administration in England*, 1946

Thurlby, M., 'Hereford cathedral: the Romanesque fabric', in *Medieval art, architecture and archaeology at Hereford,* (ed.) D. Whitehead, 1995

Torode, Brian, *The Hebrew community of Cheltenham, Gloucester and Stroud*, 1989

Underwood, Peter, *Queen Victoria's other world*, 1986

Whitehead, D., *The Castle Green at Hereford*, 2007

Whiteman, A., (ed.), *The Compton Census of 1676*, 1986

Manuscripts

Capps Roger, The cathedral church of St Mary and St Ethelbert, some aspects of its development and repair, an essay submitted to the Architectural Association Building Conservation, 1986

Cooke, William Rev, (compiled) Biographical memoirs of the custos and vicars admitted into the College at Hereford from 1660-1823, *unpublished, undated transcripts, HCA7003/4/3-4*

Dunnicliff, E., Customs and statutes of the cathedral church of Hereford, 1962, *unpublished typescript*

Lepine, D., 'Cathedrals and Society: Hereford's medieval past'. *http://www.hereford cathedral.org/ education-research/life-and-learning/Cathedrals 2010, unpublished transcript of a talk given to the Life and Learning group)*

REFERENCES

Abbreviations used

Aylmer   Aylmer G. and Tiller J. (eds.), *Hereford Cathedral, a History,* 2000

Boucher   Boucher, C., et al., *Death in the Close, a medieval mystery,* 2015

Breyer   Breyer, Betty, 'An American in Hereford', *Cantilupe Journal, no 2, Autumn 2003*

Burrow   Burrow, E.J., *Hereford Illustrated,* 1897

Cressy   Cressy, D., *Birth, marriage and death: ritual, religion, and the life-cycle in Tudor and Stuart England,* 1999

Jancey   Jancey, E.M., 'Hereford cathedral and the parish of St John the Baptist' *The Friends of Hereford cathedral annual report 1984*

Dohar   Dohar, W.J., *The Black Death and pastoral leadership, the Diocese of Hereford in the 14th century,* 1995

HAS   Hereford Archive Service

HCA   Hereford Cathedral Archives

HJ   *Hereford Journal*

HT   *Hereford Times*

Lehmberg   Lehmberg, S., *The Reformation of cathedrals: cathedrals in English society, 1485-1603,* 1988

Lobel   Lobel, Mary D., (ed.), *Historic towns-maps and plans of towns and cities in the British Isles, vol.1,* 1969

Moorman   Moorman, John, *A history of the church in England,* 1973

Torode   Torode, Brian, *The Hebrew community of Cheltenham, Gloucester and Stroud,* 1989

TWNFC   *Transactions of the Woolhope Naturalists' Field Club*

Whitehead   Whitehead, D, *The Castle Green at Hereford,* 2007

Introduction

1. To save tedious repetition in this book I refer to the parish of St John the Baptist simply as St John.

2. The history of the three other parish altars within secular cathedrals is as follows. In Lincoln, Bishop Sutton (1280-99) built 'a chapel in honour of St Mary Magdalene in the precincts of the cathedral at a suitable distance from it, where the parishioners might hear divine service'. At St Paul's, in 1671, after the great fire, the parish was united with the parish of St Augustine and there was no longer an altar in the cathedral. At Chichester there was a parish altar until the 1840s when the dean, largely at his own expense, had a Victorian gothic parish church built across the road from the cathedral. Thanks are due to the archivists of these cathedrals for this information.

3. Aylmer, p.143.

4. HCA D858/5/3 17 May 2012.

5. Other people are currently working on other histories, notably the cathedral and the parish schools, and I am therefore ignoring them in this book.

Chapter 1   Beginnings to the fall of the West end in 1786

1. Aylmer, p.70.

2. Lepine, D., *'Ande all our paresshens': secular cathedrals and parish churches in late medieval England,* 2006, p.2.

3. Lobel, p.5. St Nicholas was founded *c.*1148 and All Saints *c.*1214, with St John's then being sandwiched between these four other

city parishes. As there is no definite date for the foundation of St John's, it is not possible to be definite about the order of early parish development in the city.

4. Lepine, D., 'Cathedrals and Society: Hereford's medieval past', *(unpublished lecture for the Life and Learning series at Hereford cathedral in 2010).* See also Pearn, A.M., 'Origin and Development of urban churches and parishes: a comparative study of Hereford, Shrewsbury and Chester', *(unpublished D. Phil thesis),* 1988, p.197.

5. Jancey, E.M., 'Hereford cathedral and the parish of Saint John the Baptist', *Friends of Hereford cathedral annual report,* 1984, p.22.

6. HCA 159 *c.*1201-1208.

7. HCA 494, 1273 and 1275. See also Barrow, J., *The canons and citizens of Hereford c.1160-c.1240,* 1999, p.4.

8. Dunnicliff, E., *Customs and statutes of the cathedral church of Hereford,* 1962, p.36.

9. This was compiled to raise taxes on all ecclesiastical property in England and Wales, in order to defray the costs of an expedition to the Holy Land.

10. This area of about 24 acres included the 'King's Ditch' which probably marked the boundary between the bishop's and the king's fee.

11. Lobel, p.6. In medieval times, King Street was known as King's Ditch; East and West Streets were Behind the Wall Street and Packer's Lane respectively; Gwynne Street was Pipewell Lane; St John Street was Milk Lane; the Close was Canons Street; Church Street was Caboche or Capuchin Lane. See Pearn, pp.177-191 for a detailed discussion of the parish boundaries.

12. Bannister, A.T., *Diocese of Hereford Institutions 1539-1900,* 1923, p.124.

13. The outlying areas appear occasionally in the records, but there is too little material to make a coherent story for this book.

14. Barrow, J.S., *Fasti ecclesiae Anglicanae 1066-1300, vol.8,* 2002. See pp.41 and 43.

15. Whitehead, p.17.

16. *HT* 26 April 1919.

17. Horn, J.M., revised Lepine, D., 'Hereford Diocese', *Fasti ecclesiae Anglicanae 1300-1541,* 2009, p.xxii. See also Lepine D., *Cathedrals and society,* p.2.

18. Lepine, D., *A brotherhood of canons serving God,* 1995, p.6.

19. Barrow, J.S.*, The canons and citizens of Hereford c.1160-c.1240,* 1999, p.8.

20. Boucher, p.10.

21. Duncumb, J., *Collections towards the history and antiquities of the county of Hereford, vol.1,* 1804, p.523.

22. Boucher, p.34.

23. Aylmer, p.210.

24. Thurlby, M., 'Hereford cathedral: the Romanesque fabric', *Medieval art, architecture and archaeology at Hereford,* ed. D. Whitehead, 1995, p.15. See also Capps, Roger, 'The cathedral church of St Mary and St Ethelbert, some aspects of its development and repair', *an essay submitted to the Architectural Association Building Conservation,* 1986, p.8.

25. Smith, L.T. ed., *The Itinerary of John Leland in or about the years 1535-1543* parts IX, X and XI, 1910, p.163. The Latin is as follows: *'ad capellam joannis baptistae ejusdem ecclesiae'.* In *The register of Thomas de Cantilupe,* 1906, p.lii, Griffiths states that 'Leland alone mentions the altar of St John'.

26. Marshall, G., 'The shrine of St Thomas de Cantilupe in Hereford cathedral', *TWNFC, 1930, pp.34-50.*

27. Barrow, J.S.*, The canons and citizens of Hereford c.1160-c.1240,* 1999, p.12.

28. Lepine, D., 'Cathedrals and Society', p.6.

29. Edwards, Kathleen, *The English secular cathedrals in the Middle Ages,* 1967, p.56.

30. By the early 16th century, 22 chantries had been founded at various altars in the cathedral, see Aylmer, p.446.

31. Lehmberg, p.32.

32. *Doctrinal of Sapience,* fol.63v., quoted in Duffy, Eamon, *The Stripping of the Altars,* 1992, p.113.

33. Barrow, J.S., *Fasti ecclesiae Anglicanae 1066-1300,* 2002, p.120.

34. This is probably John Baker, alias Salwarpe, who appears to have been the vicar from *c.*1386 until at least 1399. He might even

have served until 1423 when he is referred to as a 'former vicar' (HCA 1423).

35. Capes, W.W. ed., The *register of John Trefnant, Bishop of Hereford 1389-1404*, p.20.

36. Parry, J.H. ed., *The register of Robert Mascall, Bishop of Hereford 1404-1416*, 1916, p.vii. The actual siting of this proposed chapel is unknown.

37. Marshall, G., *Hereford cathedral: its evolution and growth, c.*1951, p.174.

38. Bannister, A.T., ed., *The register of Charles Bothe, bishop of Hereford (1516-1535)*, 1921, p.365.

39. Barrow, J.S., *The canons and citizens of Hereford c.1160- c.1240*, 1999, p.9.

40. Dohar, p.35.

41. Parry, J.H., ed., *The register of John de Trilleck 1344-1361*, 1910, p.148.

42. Stone, R. and Appleton-Fox, N., *A view from Hereford's past: a report on the archaeological excavation in Hereford cathedral Close in 1993*, 1996.

43. Dohar, p.60.

44. HCA 2227.

45. Klausner, D.N., ed., *Records of early English drama: Herefordshire and Worcestershire*, 1990, p.12.

46. For a history of the vicars choral see Barrett, P., *The College of Vicars Choral at Hereford cathedral*, 1980.

47. HCA R/630.

48. Aylmer, p.69.

49. Aylmer, p.443.

50. As not all the parish vicars are mentioned in the text, an appendix gives as complete a list as can be traced from the records. There are many gaps when records are missing.

51. Parry, J., *The register of John Gilbert (1375-1389)*. See p.126 which refers to John Bakere, alias Salwarpe, vicar of Saint John in Hereford cathedral, 12 June 1386.

52. Moorman, p.83.

53. Dohar, p.39.

54. Dohar, p.49.

55. HCA 1154, 6 May 1407.

56. HCA 184, 1 January 1423/4. William Maxey had died by 1459. See HCA 162.

57. Bannister, A.T., *The register of Thomas Spofford, Bishop of Hereford, 1422-1448*, 1917, p.8.

58. HCA 3204, 31 July 1444. A mark was worth 13 shillings and 4 pence.

59. HCA 7031/1 fol 40r, 23 and 24 July 1527.

60. Lehmberg, p.68.

61. Lehmberg, p.101.

62. HCA 7031/1fol 102v, 9 May 1550.

63. Aylmer, pp.91 and 92.

64. HCA 5755. Transcribed from MS 120, pp.516-22 at Corpus Christi College, Cambridge.

65. This would be about £10 in today's money.

66. HCA 7002/1/1, 1591. The recusants in the parish would all appear to have been Catholic, rather than Puritan.

67. HCA 7002/1/1, 1591.

68. HAS HD4/1/162.

69. HCA 7031/3 p.39, 23 June 1599.

70. Sacks 19/349, 1636.

71. Sacks 19/365, 1636.

72. Bannister, A.T., *The cathedral church of Hereford, its history and constitution*, 1924, p.98.

73. Firth, C.H., *Acts and ordinances of the Interregnum, 1642-1660*, 1911, pp.840-841.

74. Sacks 22/14, 1645.

75. Shoesmith, R., *The Civil War in Hereford*, 1995, p.142.

76. HCA R609, Clavigers accounts.

77. Whitehead, p.49.

78. Lobel, p.10.

79. Sacks 25/170, 1662.

80. HCA 4675, 25 February 1670.

81. HCA 4662/3.

82. Whiteman, A., (ed.), *The Compton Census of 1676*, 1986, p.251.

83. Aylmer, p.121.

84. HCA7003/4/4 No.15. Cooke, William Rev, (compiled), *Biographical memoirs of the custos and vicars admitted into the College at Hereford from 1660-1823*, undated.

85. HCA 4604.

86. HCA 4606.

87. Lehmberg, S., *Cathedrals under siege, cathedrals in English society, 1600- 1770*, 1996, p.107.

88. HCA 7003/4/4 No. 36.
89. HCA 5174/26, April 1718.
90. Aylmer, p.455.
91. These bear the inscription St John the Baptist Hereford, Joseph Guest, AM, vicar, Fra^{co} Woodcock, John Darke, churchwardens. The hallmark is London and the date c.1760. They are 23.6 cms high and weigh 16 ozs each.
92. HCA 5715/1/40.
93. HCA 7031/4 p.123, 21 November 1726.
94. HCA 3597/1, 8 August 1772.
95. HCA 7031/5 p.8, 25 June and 10 August 1772.
96. HCA 7031/5 p.270, 5 January 1790.
97. HCA 7003/4/4 No.56.
98. HCA 7031/4 p.274, 5 June 1790.
99. Barrett, P. 'Hereford cathedral in the 19th century', *The Friends of Hereford Cathedral Annual Report,* 1986, p.14.
100. Aylmer, p.455.
101. *Pugh's Hereford Journal,* 4 April 1771.
102. HCA 7003/4/4 No. 63.
103. HCA 7031/16 p.40, 13 June 1786.
104. Aylmer, p.143.

Chapter 2   Life in the Parish to the fall of the West end

1. Moorman, p.153.
2. Cressy, p.101.
3. HCA D858/1/1 p.134.
4. HCA D858/1/1 pp.24-25.
5. HCA D858/1/1 pp.72, 80, 82.
6. HCA D858/1/2 p.54.
7. HCA D858/1/6 p.3. This was renamed the East Yorkshire Regiment in 1881.
8. HCA D858/1/2 p.5.
9. HCA D858/1/2 p.63.
10. Cross, J.L. and Livingstone, E.A. (eds)., *The Oxford dictionary of the Christian church,* 2005, p.56.
11. HCA D858/1/1 p.107.
12. Cressy, p.350.
13. Bannister, A.T., *The register of Richard Mayew Bishop of Hereford 1504-1516,* 1919, pp.167 and 221.
14. This is now a private house known as *Castle Cliffe.* It still stands on Castle Green.
15. HCA D858/1/4 p.68.
16. Whitehead, p.68.
17. Cressy, p.432.
18. Tarlow, S., *Ritual, belief and the dead in early modern Britain and Ireland,* 2011, p.136.
19. HCA D858/1/2 p.78.
20. HCA D858/1/3 p.21.
21. HCA D858/1/2 p.79.
22. HAS BG/11/7.
23. HCA D858/1/1 p.14. Haywood forest was an extra-parochial district, without a church of its own. As it was adjacent to St John's parish, burials etc. would take place in the parish 'church'.
24. Sacks 18/272 234.
25. HCA D858/1/1 p.7.
26. HCA D858/1/1 p. 27.
27. HCA D858/2 pp.27, 28, 55, 59.
28. HCA 5256/15.
29. HCA D858/3 pp.76 and D858/4 p.18.
30. HCA 7031/1 fol 64v 4 March 1530. The offices were matins, lauds, prime, terce, sext, none, vespers and compline.
31. Sacks 24/30 1661.
32. Sacks 18/331 1635.
33. Distraint: a legal term meaning the seizure of goods. OED.
34. Johnson, R., *The ancient customs of the city of Hereford,* p.139. The name of the vicar at the time is not known.
35. Sacks 4/114 1628.
36. Sacks 20/59 and 20/66 1641.
37. HCA 5247 1705.
38. HCA 5561b 1749.
39. HCA 5563 1751.
40. Sacks 15/72 1624.
41. Sacks 20/21 1637.
42. Sacks 18/252 1634.
43. Sacks 23/396 1658.
44. Sacks 3/24 1577.
45. Sacks 22/280 1656.
46. Sacks 4/89 1662.
47. Sacks 26/284 1663.
48. Sacks 4/108 1628.
49. Sacks 28/70 1634.
50. See Tate, W.E., *The parish chest: a study of the records of parochial administration in England,* 1946. There were two almshouses in the parish, St Ethelbert's and Coningsby

Hospital, but both catered to residents from the city rather than just the parish.

51. Sacks 12/253 1612.
52. Ross, *Royalist, but ... Herefordshire in the English Civil War 1640-51,* 2012, p.114.
53. Sacks 22/191 1654 and 23/324, 1658.
54. Sacks 25/114 1661.
55. Sacks 24/30 1661.
56. Sacks 25/150 1662.
57. Sacks 25/150 1662.
58. Sacks 1/347 1666.
59. Sacks 28/12 1669.
60. Sacks 1/363 1666.
61. Sacks 28/11 1669.
62. Capes, W.W., *The vicarage of St John the Baptist,* 1915, p.4.
63. HCA D858/11/2.

Chapter 3 From the fall of the West end to the dissolution of the Parish

1. Jancey, p.26.
2. HCA 7031/5 p. 277, 11 September 1790.
3. Rees, W.J., *The Hereford Guide,* 1806, p.111.
4. HCA 7031/16 p.354, 12 May 1796.
5. Britton, John, *The history and antiquities of the cathedral church of Hereford,* 1831, p.50.
6. Jancey, p.26.
7. Brasenose College had, in 1679, been given an endowment by Sarah Seymour, Duchess of Somerset which provided a number of 'Somerset' scholarships, enabling boys from Hereford Cathedral School to study there.
8. Smyth, Charles, *Cyril Forster Garbett, Archbishop of York,* 1959, p.28.
9. HCA 7031/18 12 February 1822.
10. HCA D858/7 1 3 April 1834.
11. *HJ* 8 April 1840.
12. *HJ* 25 March 1840.
13. *HJ* 20 January 1858.
14. HCA 7031/20 p.19, 25 June 1844.
15. *HJ* 18 December 1844.
16. HCA 7031/20 pp.150-153, 14 November 1848.
17. HCA 7031/20 p.169, 26 March 1849.
18. Lascelles & Co., *Directory and Gazetteer of Hereford 1851,* p.14.
19. HCA 7031/20 p.296, 26 June 1854.
20. HCA 7031/20 p.507, 10 November 1859.
21. *HT* 28 January 1860.
22. http://www.oxforddnb.com/view/article/11112?docPos=2.
23. *HT* 6 October 1877.
24. Roberts, G., *The shaping of modern Hereford,* 2001, p.114 and HCA D858/7/1, 29 March 1866.
25. *HT* 2 February 1861.
26. HCA D858/8/2, 13 October 1863.
27. *HT* 27 May 1865.
28. HCA D858/8/3, May 1866.
29. *Diocesan Calendar, 1866,* p.121. It is not clear where this door was. This report also notes that 'the mortuary chapel at Blackmarston is being enlarged ... for the special use of the poor of the parish'.
30. Moorman, p.363.
31. HCA 7031/21 p.356, 16 February 1869.
32. HCA 7031/21 p.6, 18 January 1872.
33. HCA 7031/21 pp.414-5, 27 July 1870.
34. HCA 7031/21 p.24, 24 October 1872.
35. *Western Mail,* 10 November 1873.
36. Aylmer, p.162.
37. *London Daily News,* 27 May 1876.
38. *Worcester Journal,* 26 August 1876.
39. *Leicester Journal,* 12 April 1872.
40. *Leamington Spa Courier,* 29 June 1872.
41. *Morning Post,* 26 November 1873.
42. HCA 7031/22 p.111, 12 November 1874.
43. *Western Times,* 28 September 1876.
44. Julia Cecilia Lucy 4 January 1874 and Mary Louisa Clemence 12 November 1876.
45. *HT* 6 October 1877.
46. HCA 7031/22 p. 230, 17 November 1877.
47. *Diocesan Year Book,* 1882, p.125.
48. *Diocesan Year Book,* 1885, p.131.
49. HCA 7031/22 p. 482, 7 December 1885. A lay clerk was a layman employed to sing in the cathedral choir.
50. *HT* 23 January 1886.
51. HCA D858/7/1, 19 February 1886.
52. *Birmingham Daily Post,* 15 October 1886. Also *Worcestershire Chronicle* 16 October 1886.
53. A fabric screen behind the altar in place of a reredos.
54. *Diocesan Year Book,* 1887. It was made at the East Grinstead School of embroidery.

55. HCA 7031/23 pp. 4-5, 11 November 1886.
56. *HT* 29 December 1900.
57. HCA D858/7/1, 12 October 1899.
58. *HT* 4 April 1918.
59. *London Gazette,* 15 April 1919 reported on a meeting based on Section 26 of the Pluralities Act, 1838.
60. Eales-White, J.C., *Records of Hereford cathedral school,* 1931, p.3.
61. HCA D858/12/1, 30 April 1924, parochial church council minute book.
62. HCA D858/12/1, 12 April 1926, parochial church council minute book.
63. On 28 March 1972 it was noted that marriages could be solemnised in the cathedral for certain categories of people who were connected with the cathedral and also that 'marriages of persons resident in the parish of St John shall be solemnised in the Lady Chapel'.
64. HCA D858/5/3, 17 May 2012.

Chapter 4   Life in the Parish to its dissolution

1. Aylmer, p.108.
2. *The Herefordian*, April 1910, p.10. Thanks to Howard Tomlinson for this information.
3. The Hereford Museum has no record of this painting.
4. HCA D858/1/15 p.10.
5. *Herefordshire Magazine,* February 1908, p.495.
6. 1871 census.
7. *HT* 28 March 1874.
8. HCA D858/1/12 p.153.
9. This was closed *c.*1866 when burials took place in the new city burial ground.
10. *HT* 15 September 1832.
11. *HJ* 28 November 1860.
12. During the Napoleonic Wars, there were two battles of Copenhagen in which the British were deployed, one in 1801 and the second in 1807.
13. *HJ* 6 October 1866.
14. HCA D858/1/18 pp. 72, 83, 93 and D858/1/19 pp.11 and 19.
15. There is no-one of that name in either the 1871 or 1881 census at the hotel; nor does the local newspaper give any information.
16. HAS K42/226.
17. *HT* 9 January 1841; also see *HJ* 20 January 1841.
18. *HT* 16 January 1841.
19. HCA D858/1/17 p.63.
20. *HT* 16 January 1841. This records that the funeral took place on 'Tuesday last' and a John Pugh, aged 16 was buried that day. See HCA D858/1/17 p.66.
21. Quite why he was being marched across the bridge is not clear in the newspaper account!
22. *HT* 24 July 1841.
23. *London Gazette,* 1851, p.723.
24. HAS ALS 13/4, *Will and probate of Benjamin Jennings of King Street, Hereford, statuary, 21st July 1856.*
25. Burrow, p.19.
26. E-mail from Elizabeth Patrick, 2 April 2010. See also 'The Pritchards: a family of Herefordshire Photographers' in *A Herefordshire Miscellany* (2000), pp.138-152.
27. Now the offices of Gabbs the solicitors.
28. Burrow, p.44.
29. *HT* 7 April 1860.
30. *HT* 30 July 1898.
31. Although in the parish, the cathedral school educated children from a wide area and is not included here.
32. *HJ* 3 January 1831.
33. *HT* 3 January 1852.
34. HCA 7031/21 p.246, 24 March 1866.
35. HCA D858/14/1, 26 March 1872.
36. Diocesan Calendar, 1871, p.143.
37. 1891 census.
38. HCA 7031/20 p.220, 24 March 1851.
39. HCA 7007 Hebdomadary's Book p.454.
40. HCA 7031/20 p.237, 8 December 1851. Approximately £15 today.
41. HCA 7031/20 p.243, 24 March 1852. This would be approximately £40 in today's money.
42. *HT* 12 June 1852.
43. See *John Venn and the Friends of the Hereford Poor* by Jean O'Donnell, 2007 for an excellent description of the problems of poverty, poor sanitation, etc. in mid-19th century Hereford.

44. HCA 5709, 1798.
45. *HJ* 25 October 1809.
46. Powell, J., *Hard times in Herefordshire, the effects of the workhouse and the New Poor Law*, 2008, p.4.
47. HCA D858/7/1, 8 April 1824.
48. HCA D858/7/1, 12 May 1824.
49. HCA D858/7/1, 4 August 1824.
50. HCA D858/7/1, 20 November 1828.
51. HCA D858/7/1, 27 July 1832.
52. *HT* 22 May 1841.
53. HAS BG11/17/67.
54. Powell, *op.cit.* p.96. The workhouse was in existence by 1810 as in 1832, Mrs Hall described herself as the retired matron of the workhouse, being there from 1810-1816, *HJ,* 9 May 1832.
55. Morrill, Sylvia A., 'Poor Law in Hereford 1836-1851', *TWNFC*, 1974, vol. XLI, pp.239-252. In 1838 all the inmates of St John's were transferred to the new workhouse.
56. HCA D858/7/1, 15 September 1824.
57. HCA D858/7/1, 15 September 1824.
58. HCA D858/7/1, 1 March 1825.

Chapter 5   The Silversmith, the Recluse & the Bank Manager

1. Setterfield. Diane, *The Thirteenth Tale,* 2006, p.16.
2. Information provided by Lady Ann Hoskyns.
3. 1841 census.
4. *Cheltenham Chronicle*, 26 November 1812.
5. Torode, p.24.
6. *HJ* 27 July 1825.
7. *HJ* 12 July 1826.
8. Torode, p.21.
9. *HJ* 13 April 1831.
10. *HT* 9 January 1836. Nothing has been found in the transportation lists so they might have escaped this fate.
11. *HT* 21 August 1841.
12. My thanks go to the late Michael Webber who gave me the information on this headstone.
13. *HJ* 22 January 1840.
14. *HJ* 22 April 1840.
15. *HJ* 3 June 1840.
16. Torode, p.36.
17. *HJ* 24 December 1845; *HT* 20 December 1845.
18. *Clocks,* December 1990, p.39. See also Branson, T. and Eisel, J. *Herefordshire clockmakers and watchmakers*, 2005.
19. Burke, Sir B. *Genealogical and Heraldic Dictionary of the Peerage and Baronetcy, 42nd ed.*1880, p.650.
20. *The Herefordshire Magazine,* no date, p.494.
21. Bryson, Bill, *At Home,* 2010 p.136.
22. *HJ* 19 April 1826.
23. *HJ* 19 October 1836.
24. *HJ* 18 May 1842.
25. *HJ* 19 March 1845.
26. *HT* 19 December 1835.
27. *HT* 14 December 1839. This church still stands at the junction of Barton Road and Friar Street, replacing one that stood inconveniently in the junction of King Street and Bridge Street.
28. *HJ* 10 October 1855.
29. HAS BC64, nos.18 and 198.
30. *HT* 14 May 1859.
31. *HJ* 13 December 1862.
32. http://www.oxforddnb.com/view/article/18345.
33. *HJ* 7 February 1849.
34. *HT* 4 July 1863.
35. *HJ* 8 August 1863.
36. Humfrys, W.J., *Memories of old Hereford,* 1924, pp.6 and 22.
37. *HJ* 6 October 1866.
38. *Pall Mall Gazette,* 21 October 1878.
39. Matthews, Frederick, *Fragments and fancies,* 2011.
40. *Bristol Mercury,* 3 June 1880.
41. *Bath Chronicle and Weekly Gazette,* 18 January 1883.

Chapter 6   The Clairvoyant, the Manure Manufacturer & the Dancing Master

1. Pym, Barbara, *No fond return of love. http://www.telegraph.co.uk/culture/books/10071305.html.*
2. *HT* 20 April 1844.
3. The census for 1841 at St Columb Major in Cornwall lists Barnard Eagle with a wife,

Jane, a daughter Georgiana, aged six and a son, George, aged three.

4. By 1851 the family were in Glastonbury, with two more children of the marriage.

5. *HJ* 27 March 1844.

6. *HT 20 December 1851.*

7. *HT 27 December 1851.*

8. E-mail from Michael Hunter, curator Osborne House, 7 May 2015.

9. *Victoria's other world,* 1986, p.107.

10. *Western Times* 16 November 1850.

11. The information on George Eagle comes from an article by Stephen Butt in an electronic newsletter *Psypioneer* ed. P. Grant, vol. 1 nos. 15-16, July/August 2005 pp.175-194.

12. *The Star*, Guernsey 20 May 1858.

13. *The Ipswich Journal* 22 May 1858.

14. I am grateful to Dr Henry Connor for supplying much useful information on Andrew Rowan's career.

15. *HT* 4 April 1846.

16. The Woolhope Club was founded in 1851 as the *Woolhope Naturalists Field Club*. It still meets and publishes its *Transactions* annually with articles on natural history, geology, history and archaeology.

17. *HT* 3 April 1847.

18. *HT* 11 December 1847, 25 December 1847.

19. *HT* 22 January 1848.

20. *HT* 5 June 1847. He has another letter on agricultural issues in the *Times* of 6 November 1852 and one on the sanitary condition of Hereford on 29 January 1853.

21. *HT* 22 April 1848.

22. *HT* 28 October 1848.

23. *HT* 17 February 1849.

24. Roberts, G., *The shaping of modern Hereford*, 2001, p.108.

25. *HT* 16 February 1850.

26. *HT* 30 November 1850.

27. *HT* 29 March 1851.

28. *HT* 19 April 1851.

29. *HT* 10 May 1851.

30. *HT* 12 July 1851.

31. *HT* 26 July 1851.

32. *HT* 14 February 1852.

33. *HT* 28 February 1852.

34. *HT* 8 May 1852.

35. *HT* 5 June 1852.

36. *HT* 12 March 1853.

37. *HT* 7 October 1854.

38. *HT* 16 February 1856.

39. *HT* 3 October 1857.

40. *Scarborough Gazette,* several advertisements between 1859 and 1869.

41. *HT* 17 September 1864.

42. The LSA is no longer awarded but was the Licence of the Society of Apothecaries; the LRCP, also no longer awarded, was the Licentiate of the Royal College of Physicians; whilst the LFPS was the Licentiate of the Royal College of Surgeons.

43. Information supplied by Dr Henry Connor from *The Lancet,* 24 January 1891, p.233.

44. He was 79 when he was buried on 10 September 1891.

45. In fact he was there in the 1841 census, again giving the wrong age to the enumerator.

46. Robert Vaughan seems to be as muddled about his birth place as his age. In 1871 and 1891 he gives Hereford as his place of birth; in 1881 Wales. If he and his father were of Welsh origin, and given their name, this seems very likely, no doubt some anti-Welsh prejudice was at work here.

47. *HT* 1 April 1848.

48. *HT* 24 July 1847.

49. *HJ* 20 July 1853.

50. http://archiver.rootsweb.ancestry.com/ th/read/WILDING/2001-08/0997825827. The same posting gives Elizabeth's address in 1881 as Gwynne Street, Hereford. The marriage took place on 21 June 1859 in Breinton , entry no 149, register no 1. Information from Phil Bufton Hereford Family History Society.

51. *HJ* 17 April 1861.

52. Francis died in December 1876 aged 8.

53. Dickens, Charles, *Bleak House,* http://www. gutenberg.org/files/1023/1023-h/1023-h.htm.

Chapter 7 The Slave Owner & the Governess

1. Breyer, p.9.

2. CRO ST 853/3, letter from G. Margry to J.S. Stephens, 1 Jan 1949. Gertrude Margry was

a cousin, and John Sturges Stephens a second cousin.

3. Breyer, p.11.
4. Leigh, F. *Ten years on a Georgia plantation since the war,* 1883, p. xvii.
5. A type of musical entertainment, originally outdoors, where popular music was performed. They were generally light-hearted, sometimes risqué, even bawdy.
6. HCA 6492 Handwritten diary. I have transcribed it as it is written with its occasional idiosyncrasies of grammar and spelling.
7. HCA 6492.
8. In Polish Dziewicka is used for females but many Poles only use the male version to avoid confusion and it is this version I will use here.
9. Numbers 9 and 10 are now Penn House, offices used by a number of individuals and companies, including Jesse Norman, the MP for Hereford and South Herefordshire.
10. There are no records relating to their teaching careers in the Somerset archives.
11. John Hanbury.
12. Dziewicki, G., *Glimpses of Polish Life in Town and Country Pre-War to 1914*, 1937, p.8.
13. Waysblum, M., 'The Catholic Boys at Ackworth: from letters before and after their time there,' *Journal of the Friends Historical Society, vol 44, 1952*, pp.70-78.
14. CRO ST/873. All the photographs and drawings are also from this archive.
15. *HT* 12 July 1851.
16. *HT* 19 June 1852.
17. *HT* 18 February 1854.
18. *HT* 25 February 1854.
19. CRO ST/821, Theodore to Mary 7 November 1869.
20. CRO ST/821, Theodore to Mary 30 July 1869.
21. *HT* 19 July 1862.
22. I am grateful to Peter Thorpe, at the National Railway Museum for his help in deciphering the intricacies of Bradshaw's timetable.
23. All quotes from the *Hereford Times*, 27 December 1862. The photograph of Severin Dziewicki was found amongst the archives for St Michaels College, Tenbury so he might well have been teaching there but there but there is no definite evidence to support this theory. The college was founded in 1856 by Sir Frederick Gore Ouseley, precentor at Hereford cathedral, to 'promise a course of training and to form a model, for the daily choral services of the Church in these realms, and, for the furtherance of this object, to receive, educate and train boys in religious, secular and musical knowledge' http://www.bodley.ox.ac.uk/dept/scwmss/wmss/online/1500-1900/st-michaels-college/st-michaels-college.html). (http://www.smcsociety.co.uk/thecollege.html).
24. Email from Sue Jones, Leominster Priory office, 27 November 1012.
25. This map is dated 1986.
26. A footnote in Waysblum, p.78.
27. Although both sisters worked in Poland for many years, they rarely seemed to meet.
28. CRO ST/806. Extracts from Gertrude Dziewicka's 'Happenings: reminiscences of Hereford' written for her cousin Jeanette Cadbury in memory of her mother Ethel Southall, with special reference to her ancestors of the Evans family.
29. E-mail from Christine Gladwin, Sidcot School, 12 November 2011. It is clear from the Minutes of the School Committee that Gertrude was not a member of the Quakers, but that she was a regular attender at the Hereford Meeting, under the care of her aunt.
30. Christine Gladwin, secretary of Sidcot writes that 'good pieces of work were put into a volume each year when the Quakers of the Southwest came to check that the work was up to standard'. Email 1 June 2012.
31. CRO/ST 822. All the Kanie letters are from this file.
32. CRO/ST/822/210.
33. All the 'revolution' letters are from ST/824 in the CRO.
34. It is not clear from Gertrude's letters whether she ever mastered the language, for French was the *lingua franca* among educated Poles.
35. CRO/ST 826 9 August 1914.
36. CRO/ST 852.
37. CRO/ST 852 22 February 1945, Richard Smith to J.S. Stephens.

38. This was renamed Belle Orchard House after 1930 when it changed from being a workhouse.
39. CRO/ST/853/10 Symonds, solicitor to J.S. Stephens.
40. 86 Ledbury 9a 75.
41. CRO/ST/854.
42. 8184 headstone in situ, granite, Hereford City cemetery. I am grateful to Phil Bufton of Hereford Family History Society for this information. See Also HCA 6482 H.1S/E MD G.

Appendix

1. Parry, J., *The Register of John Gilbert Bishop of Hereford (1375-1389)*, 1913, p.126, 12 June 1386.
2. Capes, W., *The Register of John Trefnant, Bishop of Hereford (1389-1401)*, 1914, p.58, 7 November 1393.
3. Bannister, A.T., *The Register of Thomas Spofford, Bishop of Hereford (1422-1448)*, 1917, p.8, 1422.
4. Parry, J.H., *The Register of John Stanbury, Bishop of Hereford (1453-1474)*, 1918, p.46, 20 December 1457.
5. Havergal, F., *Fasti herefordenses & other antiquarian memorials of Hereford*, 1869, p.96. The dates for Havergal entries are from the year of election to the year of death.
6. Havergal, p.96.
7. *ibid*, p.96.
8. *ibid*, p.97.
9. *ibid*, p.100.
10. *ibid*, p.101.

Index of Names

Aelfgar, son of earl of Mercia 1
Amphlett, Thomas, of Droitwich 15
Anderson, Mr, chiropodist 58
Andrews, John, soldier 21
    Robert, dishonest overseer 37-38
Argest, Ann, charwoman 70
Arkwright, John 58
Athelstan, Bishop 1
Atlay, Bishop James 36
Aylestone, Francis 22

Bagnall, Mrs, pauper 53
Baker, alias Salwarpe, John 9, 91
Baldwin, William, thief 56
Ballard, John, recusant 12
Bally, Louise, maid 41
Baughan, John, vicar 91
Berrington, Ottwell & Margaret 27
Berthold, Marc, coachman 41
Birch, Colonel John 13
    Thomas, labourer 56
Bisse, Bishop 16
Bodenham, Charles 81
Borsley, Elianor, pauper 26
Bosworth, William, overseer 27
Boulton, Thomas, of the Globe 49-50
Boughan, John, vicars choral 13
Bowdley, Mary 80
Bradford, William, foreman 49-50
Bradley, William, monk & vicar 9, 91
Brooke, Elizabeth, recusant 12
Brookes, William, servant 45
Bryant, Julia & Richard, paupers 54
Brystow, Thomas, curate 10, 91
Bull, Dr & Mrs Henry Graves 38
Bustin, Mr, photographer 40
Butler, Pierce, slave owner 73

Catton, Thomas, comedian 23
Capel, Alfred, vicar 37-38, 91
Carless, Joseph, town clerk 39
Carpenter, Thomas, schoolmaster 51

Caxton, William 6
Charles I 13, 24
Chave, William, chemist 47
Clark, Isaac, of Bromyard 25
    Thomas 21
Clarke, William, Close constable 52
Coke, John 23
Combe, John, of Whitbourne 21
Cooke, Alice, apple seller 23
    William, wool stapler 45
Cox, Thomas, soldier 20
Credenhill, William, chaplain 9, 91
Cross, Hubert 44
    Susan 56
Crowther, William, vicar 15-16, 91
Cutler, John & Mary 25

Davies, Morgan 71
    Thomas, seafarer 23
    Mr, coachbuilder 70
    William, servant of 22
Davies family (of 1611) 20
Dawes, Dean Richard 32
de Aigueblanche, Bishop Peter 5
de Hanwelle, Robert, vicar 9, 91
de Leominster, Walter, vicar 91
Dovey, Alice & Ethel 74-75
Drury, Anne Lucy 68
    Charles William 68
Dryden, Jonathan, vicar 13, 91
Duppa, Thomas 25
Dutton, William 42
Dyke, Elizabeth 21
Dziewicki, Gertrude Elizabeth 73, 77-88
    Henry 78, 81, 82, 83
    Jane 77-82
    Joseph (Roman) 79, 81, 82
    Mary 79, 81, 82, 83
    Severin 77-81
    Theodore 79, 81, 82

Eagle, George Bernard, clairvoyant 63-65
    George, son of George Bernard 63
    Georgiana 63, 65
    Hannah 63
Edwards, Hannah 63
Edwin, Benjamin 22
Edward III, visit of 7
Edwards, Miss 17
Evans, George, potboy 50

Floyd, Mr & Mrs Edward 14

Garbett, James, vicar 30-31, 91
   family of 30-31
Garstone, Mary, servant 50
Gawens, Lawrence, pauper 26
Goetz, Robert, schoolmaster 41
Goss, John, vicar 32-37, 51, 91
      marriage mystery 36
   Sir John, composer 32
   Lucy 36-37
Grainger, Mary, servant 46
Griffiths, Richard 25
Guest, Joseph, vicar 16-17, 91
Gwillim, Thomas, vicar 14, 91
Gwyn, David 22

Haliday, Robert, vicar general 10
Hampden, Bishop Renn 33
Hanbury, John, vicar 31-32, 91
Harper, John, shoemaker & overseer 27
Harris, Simon, Jane & family 27
Hart, A.S., dentist 57
Hartland, William, pauper 36
Hatfort, William 27
Hatton, Brian 41
   Charles, baker 51
Hayward, Jane 25
Henry VII, visit of 8
Herbert, Austin, overseer 71
Hill, Mary, servant 46
   William, sergeant of the king's mace 24
Hodson, Elizabeth, pauper 26
Holt, John, glover 25
Hoskyns, Catherine Mary Jane 41
   Chandos 55, 57-59
   Sir Hungerford & Sarah 41-42
   Sarah, niece of Chandos 58

Hughes, Henry, apprentice 52
   John, weaver 23

Jebb, John 35
Jenkins, Revd Canon 35
Jennings, Ann, mason 46
   Mrs, workhouse matron 53
   Benjamin 46
   William, verger 47
Jones, Annie, dealer 77, 82
   Evan, vicar
   Francis, tailor 26
   Jane 77
   Joseph, bookseller 42, 77, 80
   Lucy, spinster 25
   William, recusant 12
Jones family (of 1628) 20

Kemble, Fanny, actress 73
Kerry, James, pauper 26

Lane, Herbert, butcher 25
Laud, Archbishop William 13
Lazarus, Sarah 55
   Solomon, silversmith 55-57
Lederer, Louis, waiter 41
Le Grant, Robert 6
Legge, Richard, pauper 12
Leigh, Frances 73-77
   Dean Joseph Wentworth 39-40, 73, 74
Leland, John 5
Levi, Moses 55
   Sarah 55
Llewellyn, Anne, pauper 53
Lodges family (of 1671) 20
Lowe, William, puritan minister 13
Lynke, John 91
   widow 26

Marshall, George 5
Mason, Thomas, centenarian 27
Matthews, Frederick Hoskyns 55, 59-61
   Dr John, father of Frederick 59
   John, brother of Frederick 60
Maxey, William, vicar 9-10, 91
Meats, Alice 42-43
   John, farmer 42-43
Merewether, Dean 31, 32

Merly, Fanny, waitress 41
Mey, John, mayor 9
Mills, Mr 35
   Richard 22
Moore, Alban, sexton 3, 47
Morgan, William 28
Morris, Henry, brewer 50
   Mr & Mrs John, paupers 26
   William, 'old sailor' 42-43
Morwska, Irene Marie 81
Musgrave, Bishop Thomas 31
Mydroffe, Richard 21

Nicholson, Mrs J. 13

Oates, Nicholas, tailor 26
Oldmeadow, Mr, schoolmaster
Oswin, William, jeweller 47
Ouseley, Sir Frederick 35

Payne, Ellen 43
   William, hotel keeper 43
Pellegrino, Panacali, plaster figure maker 41
Perks, John, thief 56
Pews, Elizabeth, thief 25
Peyton, William, vicar 14, 22, 91
Phillips, Richard, Cathedral Close keeper 44
   family of 44
Philpot, Nicholas 22
Pisani, Domenico, engineer apprentice 41
Porter, Elizabeth 53
Powell, Elizabeth, charwoman 42
   Gerram, 'stroller' 23
Preece, Elizabeth 45
Price, Thomas, dau. of 28
   widow, pauper 54
Prichard, John, recusant 14
Prichot, John, cooper 14
Primrose, George, puritan minister 13
Pritchard, Walter, tailor 47-48
Prophete, Dean John 7
Pugh, John 44
   Thomas & Ann 44-45
Pye, Miss, schoolmistress 82

Ralph the Timid, Earl 1
Rawlins, Thomas 27
Richard II 8

Richards, John 24
Rivington, Revd Luke 34
Robert, vicar 91
Robinson, Richard 43
   Walter Byatt 42-43
Rodd, James 27
Rogers, Amos, anabaptist 21
   Roger, vicar 10, 91
   Major Wroth 27
Rowan, Andrew, manure manufacturer 63, 65-69
   family of 65, 68
   Ann Lucy 68
   Charles 69
   Sarah 65, 68
Rowlands, Phoebe, schoolmistress 51

Savaker, Magdalen 25
Scory, Bishop John 11-12
Scott, Gilbert 33
Sergeant, William, murderer 23
Sexty, Elizabeth 47
Simmes, Frances & Elizabeth 14
Skynner, Philip, vicar 12, 91
Smith, C.S., of Ledbury Social Welfare
   Institution 87
   Mary 21
   Richard, secretary to Quakers 86-87
Speth, George William 376
   Lucy 36-37
Stephens, John Sturge 86-87
Swinfield, Bishop 5

Taylor, Silas 4
Thackeray, Leonard, actor 47
Thomas, John 27
   John, of Coningsby Hospital 43-44
   William, feltmaker 21
Thorp, Eliza 25
Tonkins, William, soldier 20
Traherne, Henry 27
   John 23
Trefnant, Bishop Hugh 6-7
Tryst, Herbert & Matilda 22
Tudor, James, overseer 27

Underwood, Richard, vicar 17-18, 30, 91

Vaughan, Elizabeth 71
    Robert, cooper 63, 69-72
        family of 71
    Robert, father of Robert 70
Victoria, Queen 64-65

Walwyn, Nicholas, canon 24
Walters, John & Alice, charity founders 28
Watkins, Mr & Mrs Henry, thief 53
Wharton, William, pauper 53

White, Sarah, pauper 53
Wilding, Elizabeth 71
William, 'canon and chaplain' 2, 91
Williams, Francis, servant 21
    Mary, widow 27
    sisters, of the Mitre 49
    William 22
Wilkes, Thomas, chair maker 52
Wynstanley, Margery 21

General Index

Anabaptists 21

Black Death 7, 9

Civil War 13-14
Confraternity of the Blessed Sacrament, the 37

Declaration of Indulgence 14
Doctrinal of Sapyence 6

English Church Union, the 35, 37

Glorious Revolution 14

Hereford
  bishop's fee 2
  Cathedral
    Anglo-Saxon origins 1
    churchyard 29
    Close, used for immoral behaviour 52
      constable 52
    crypt 5
    damage in 1055 5
    Lady Chapel 32, 33, 37, 38-39, 40
    north transept 5, 30, 31
      pews 32
    Portland Street 79
    rebuilding, 12th-century 4
    restoration 1800s 31, 32
    School 79
    services in 6
    St Ethlebert, cult of 5
    St Thomas Cantilupe, cult & shrine of 5-6, 7-8, 11
    West front, collapse of 18, 30
  canonical houses 3
  City and County Bank 59-61
  city burial ground 33, 87-88
  Tailors Guild 26
  House of Correction 21-22
  parish formation 1

St John's parish 1-3
  altar, place in cathedral 1, 5-6, 30, 31, 32, 33, 37, 38-39, 40
    maintenance of 6
  baptisms 19-21, 41-42
    adult 21
    illegitimate children 21, 41-42
  body snatchers 43
  burials 22-23, 29, 35-36, 43-45
    Blackmarston burial ground 29, 30, 33, 43
  card playing 23
  cattle market 48, 49
  census of 1841 41
  chalices 16
  charities 28
  Coningsby Hospital 43-44
  deaths 20, 44-45
    drowning 44
    murders 22-23
    suicide 45
    unusual 22
  detached parts 3, 39-40
  dissolution *xi*, 40,
  drunkenness 25
  education 50-51, 78, 79-80
    Commercial School, the 51
    Mrs Wright's school 50
    St John's school 51
  gambling 23
  Globe, the 49-50
  Green Dragon Hotel 79
  Gwynne Street, reputation 35, 42, 54, 77
  marriages 21-22, 42-43
  occupations of residents 23, 29, 41, 42, 45-50
  Mechanics Institute 51, 52
  Mitre, the 49
  poor, care for 22, 26-28, 52-54
    funerals 35-36, 44
  punishment 25, 51
    transportation 53, 56
  recreations 23-24

separate church, discussions 4, 31, 32, 33
slander 25
thievery 25
vicarage house 9, 10
vicars 8-9, 40
    responsibilities for services 9, 40
whoring 25, 35, 52
workhouse 42, 44, 53-54
St Owen's parish 1
St Peter's parish 1
vicars choral 13, 16, 17
high and low church 15, 34

Interregnum 13-14

John, King, quarrel with Pope Innocent 9

Leominster Priory 81
Lebury, Social Welare Institution 87

Poor Law Amendment Act 1834 53

recusancy 12-13, 14
Reformation, The 10-13, 14
Restoration, The 13-14
Rose Cottage, Aylestone Hill 79

slavery 21
Society of the Holy Cross, the 37
Society of the Holy Ghost, the 34

Woolhope Club 66

Also from Logaston Press

The Story of Hereford

Edited by Andy Johnson & Ron Shoesmith

Contributors: Keith Ray, Ron Shoesmith, PJ Pikes, David Whitehead,
Heather Hurley, Chris Pullin, Sarah Arrowsmith, Rosemary Firman,
Malcolm Thurlby, Ken Hylson-Smith, John Eisel and Derek Foxton

This book tells the story of Hereford in breadth and depth, drawing on the knowledge of a number of experts in their field to shed light on various less well-known aspects of that history, and bringing the results of recent research and archaeological investigation to a wider readership.

Some chapters cover Hereford's story in broadly chronological order, while others address particular themes. Alongside more familiar aspects of the city's history – for example, how it fared in the Civil War, the foundation and history of the cathedral, the navigation of the Wye – there is new material on Saxon Hereford, medieval trade, Georgian Hereford and the activities of freehold land societies in the Victorian period. There is also information on less well known aspects of the city's past, be it Hereford's prominence as a great centre of scientific and other learning at the end of the 1100s, the use of the city as a base by Simon de Montfort, and also by Prince Henry in the wars with Owain Glyndwr. Whether you are familiar with Hereford's history or completely new to it, there is much here to interest, intrigue and surprise.

In addition there are over 200 illustrations, most in colour, ranging from copies of pages of medieval books through watercolour and oil paintings to aerial photographs.

Paperback, 336 pages with over 160 colour and 50 mono illustrations
ISBN 978 1 906663 98 8   Price £15

Logaston Press

publishes many books about Herefordshire,
adjoining counties and the Marches of Wales

If you want to know what we have in print and what special offers we have
available at any given time, then go to: www.logastonpress.co.uk

Some titles in print (as at April 2016) are listed here:

John Venn and the Friends of the Hereford poor

Walking the old ways of Herefordshire

Herefordshire Place-names

The Archaeology of Herefordshire: An Exploration

A Dictionary of Herefordshire Biographies

Roses round the door?
Rural images, realities & responses: Herefordshire, 1830s-1930s

The Dovecotes and Pigeon Houses of Herefordshire

Shadows in the Hay
Landscape, nature and the passage of time on a Herefordshire farm

Royalist, but ... Herefordshire in the English Civil War, 1640-51

The Hidden History of Ewyas Lacy in Herefordshire

Ludford Bridge & Mortimer's Cross

Poems and Paintings of the Malvern Hills

Goodrich Castle: Its History & Buildings